This b...

how2become

A Prison Officer
The Insider's Guide

Orders: Please contact How2become Ltd, Suite 2,
50 Churchill Square Business Centre, Kings Hill,
Kent ME19 4YU.

Telephone: (44) 0845 643 1299 - Lines are open Monday to
Friday 9am until 5pm. Fax: (44) 01732 525965. You can also
order via the e mail address info@how2become.co.uk.

ISBN: 978-1907558-01-6

First published 2010

Typeset for How2become Ltd by Good Golly Design,
Canada, goodgolly.ca

Printed in Great Britain for How2become Ltd by Bell & Bain
Ltd, 303 Burnfield Road, Thornliebank, Glasgow G46 7UQ.

CONTENTS

INTRODUCTION

Dear Sir/Madam,

Welcome to how2become a Prison Officer: The Insider's Guide. This guide has been designed to help you prepare for and pass the Prison Officer selection process. You will find the guide both a comprehensive and highly informative tool for helping you obtain one of the most sought after careers available.

The job of a Prison Officer is both highly challenging and rewarding. You will need a certain set of special skills in order to carry out the role competently. As you can imagine, at times you could be dealing with some of the country's most notorious prisoner's. Being a Prison Officer is not about punishing or bullying inmates. It is about treating them correctly and rehabilitating them, ready for when they eventually return to society. This guide will help you to demonstrate the qualities that are required to become a competent prison officer. Read each section carefully and in particular learn the six core behavioural skills that are crucial to the role. If you learn these, then your chances of success

will increase dramatically.

If you would like any further assistance with the selection process then we offer the following products and training courses via the website www.how2become.co.uk:

- How to pass the Prison Officer Selection Test Role-Play DVD;

- Prison Officer Selection Test (POST) online testing facility;

- One-Day Prison Officer training course.

Finally, you won't achieve much in life without hard work, determination and perseverance. Work hard, stay focused and be what you want!

Good luck and best wishes,

The How2become team

PREFACE

By Author Richard McMunn

Before I get into the guide and teach you how to prepare for the Prison Officer selection process, it is important that I explain a little bit about my background and why I am qualified to help you succeed.

I joined the Royal Navy soon after leaving school and spent four fabulous years in the Fleet Air Arm branch onboard HMS Invincible. It had always been my dream to become a Firefighter and I only ever intended staying in the Royal Navy for the minimum amount of time. At the age of 21 I left the Royal Navy and joined Kent Fire and Rescue Service. Over the next 17 years I had an amazing career with a fantastic organisation. During that time I was heavily involved in training and recruitment, often sitting on interview panels and marking application forms for those people who wanted to become Firefighters. I also worked very hard and rose to the rank of Station Manager in a relatively short space of time. I passed numerous assessment centres during my

time in the job and I estimate that I was successful at over 95% of interviews I attended.

The reason for my success was not because I am special in any way, or that I have lots of educational qualifications, because I don't! In the build up to every job application or promotion interview I always prepared myself thoroughly. I found a formula that worked, and that is what I intend to teach you throughout the duration of this book.

Over the past few years I have taught many people how to pass the selection process for becoming a Prison Officer, both through this guide and also during my one-day intensive training course. Each and every one of the students who attends my course is determined to pass, and that is what you will need to do too if you are to be successful.

The way to pass the selection process is to embark on a comprehensive period of intense preparation. I would also urge you to use an action plan during your preparation. This will allow you to focus your mind on exactly what you need to do in order to pass. For example, if it has been many years since you last sat a test, then you may have to work very hard in order to pass the Prison Officer Selection Test (POST), which forms part of the selection process. The point I am making here is that it is within your power to improve on your weak areas. If you use an action plan then you are far more likely to achieve your goals.

I use action plans in just about every element of my work. Action plans work simply because they focus your mind on what needs to be done. Once you have created your action plan, stick it in a prominent position such as your fridge door. This will act as a reminder of the work that you need to do in order to prepare properly for selection. Your action plan might look something like this:

My weekly action plan for preparing for Prison Officer selection

Monday	Tuesday	Wednesday	Thursday	Friday
Research into the role of the Prison Service and the role of a Prison Officer. I will also study the Prison Service website.	60 minutes study in relation to the six core behavioural skills.	Check the Prison Service website for vacancies.	Research into the role of the Prison Service and the role of a Prison Officer. I will also study the Prison Service website.	60 minutes study in relation to the six core behavioural skills. 20 minutes preparation for the Language Test (RAD).
60 minutes preparation for the Prison Officer Selection Test (POST).	30 minutes learning about the Prison Service Statement of Purpose, Security procedures, Decency statement and Equality and Fairness policy.	60 minutes numerical reasoning test work and preparation for the Prison Officer Selection Test (POST).	60 minutes Role Play practice with a friend or relative concentrating on the six core behavioural skills.	60 minutes preparation for the Prison Officer Selection Test (POST).
20-minute jog or brisk walk. 30 minutes work on improving my memory.	30 minutes gym work.	20 minutes reading about the role of a Prison Officer. 30 minutes work on improving my memory.	30 minutes light gym work and bleep test.	20-minute jog or brisk walk.

Note: Saturday and Sunday, rest days.

The above sample action plan is just a simple example of what you may wish to include. The content of your action plan will very much depend on your strengths and weaknesses. After reading this guide, decide which areas you need to work on and then add them to your action plan. Areas that

you may wish to include in your action plan could be:

- Researching the role of a Prison Officer;

- Researching the training that you will undergo as a Prison Officer;

- Researching the Prison Service and what it stands for;

- Studying the Prison Service website;

- Carrying out practice tests that are similar to the ones required during the Prison Officer Selection Test (POST) and also during the Recruitment Assessment Day (RAD);

- Improving your memory in preparation for the Recalling Seen Information Test;

- Improving your reading comprehension ability;

- Fitness preparation;

- Learning the six core behavioural skills and practising the role-plays.

The aim of this guide is to teach you the importance of preparation. During my career I have been successful at over 95% of interviews and assessments that I have attended. The reason for this is simply because I always embark on a period of focused preparation, and I always aim to improve on my weak areas. I would always carry out a mock interview before I attended the real thing. This would allow me to have a go at responding to the possible interview questions I might be asked during the real thing. This in itself allowed me to improve my confidence greatly. Follow this simple process and you too can enjoy the same levels of success that I have enjoyed.

Finally, it is very important that you believe in your own abilities. It does not matter if you have no qualifications. It

does not matter if you have no knowledge yet of the role of a Prison Officer or the work that the Prison Service carries out. What does matter is self-belief, self-discipline and a genuine desire to improve and become successful.

Enjoy reading the guide and then set out on a period of intense preparation!

Best wishes,

Richard McMunn

CHAPTER I

THE ROLE OF A PRISON OFFICER

THE PRISON OFFICER

The modern day Prison Officer has an important role to play in ensuring prisoners are treated decently and humanely, encouraging them to live useful, law-abiding lives once released from custody.

Your role as a competent and effective Prison Officer stretches far further than ensuring prisoners abide to prison rules. You will be involved in their education, training and coaching, which in turn will help them to lead better lives both inside and outside of prison. Naturally there comes a great deal of reward with this role and many Prison Officers enjoy the benefits of a good salary, working conditions and, above all, job satisfaction. Yes, the role of a prison officer is demanding and challenging but being part of a team that transforms people's lives is a great prospect for many Prison Service employees. Many people apply to join the Prison

Service every year and by researching the role, the selection process and also preparing yourself fully, you will drastically improve your chances of becoming a Prison Officer.

Apart from custodial duties, you will be expected to build close relationships with those people serving custodial sentences and obviously this takes a great deal of skill, education and awareness. This type of challenge is not for everyone but if you believe you have the right qualities, attributes and a determination to succeed, then you can become a Prison Officer.

The Prison Officer's role is therefore vast and varied. On the following page I have detailed a number of the duties you can expect to perform as a qualified Prison Officer. The Prison Service recognises that the skills required to carry out this role cannot be obtained overnight and therefore, if you are successful in your application, you will receive ongoing quality training to keep you at the peak of your performance. You will also be expected to pass an annual fitness test to prove your capability and competence in your role.

THE PRISON OFFICER JOB DESCRIPTION

Custodial duties entail responsibility for the security, supervision, training and rehabilitation of people committed to prison by the courts. This includes motivating prisoners to do what is best for themselves and others around them, within a safe, decent and healthy environment. Work varies according to the type of prison and the level of security, for example category A prisoners require closer supervision than those in category C. Prison Officers must establish and maintain positive working relationships with prisoners, balancing authority with a large amount of understanding and compassion. Prison Officers need to be able to think

on their feet, making quick decisions and dealing effectively with unexpected situations.

THE MAIN DUTIES AND RESPONSIBILITIES OF A PRISON OFFICER

The main duties of a Prison Officer include:

- Carrying out security checks and searching procedures.
- Supervising the prisoners that they are responsible for.
- Maintaining order when required.
- Accounting for the whereabouts of prisoners.
- Carrying out relevant restraint procedures whenever necessary.
- Treating prisoners decently and humanely, respecting their rights when appropriate.
- Protecting prisoners from harm.
- Promoting anti-bullying and suicide prevention policies.
- Taking part in education and rehabilitation schemes for prisoners.
- Writing reports on prisoners.

PRISON OFFICER SALARY

The Prison Service offers a very generous salary. Salary progression will be on an annual basis dependent upon performance. In England and Wales, the starting salary for a Prison Officer is approximately £17,744 a year. This can rise to £26,858 a year with long service. Salaries in Scotland are between £14,877 and £19,800 a year. These figures

are intended as a guide only and are correct at the time of writing.

APPLYING TO BECOME A PRISON OFFICER

Prison Officer vacancies are usually advertised in the local media and online. The best place to check for vacancies is on the Prison Service website, which can be located here:

www.hmprisonservice.gov.uk

TRAINING TO BECOME A PRISON OFFICER

During later sections of the guide I will explain what the selection process involves and more importantly how you can pass it. Once you have successfully passed all of the different testing elements, you will undertake a comprehensive training programme, which consists of the following:

PRISON OFFICER ENTRY LEVEL TRAINING (POELT)

This initial course will last for eight weeks and it will provide you with all of the necessary skills, knowledge, information and values that you need to perform the role competently. As you can imagine, you will need lots of confidence as a Prison Officer and this will form part of your training.

POELT is usually carried out at the Prison Service College (PSC), which is based at Newbold Revel, Rugby, and also at a local POELT training centre.

The following is a breakdown of the different training and assessments you will undergo during your initial eight-week course:

Week 1 - Establishment induction

During the first week you will be placed at your allocated establishment where you will undergo an intensive induction and familiarisation programme. You will get to meet your work colleagues and also your line manager, who will explain what he/she expects from you whilst you are working there.

Weeks 2 to 7 – Prison Service College or local training centre

During this period of training you will really be put through your paces. You will get to learn lots about the role of a Prison Officer, how to carry out Control and Restraint procedures (C & R), how to work effectively as a team and you will also take part in role-play based scenarios.

During this stage you will be assessed both via written examinations and also practical assessments.

Week 8 – Return to establishment

During week 8 you will return to your allocated establishment where you will start to put into practice all that you have learnt so far. Obviously this is a very important part of your development and you will have the opportunity to learn from your work colleagues' knowledge and expertise too.

Once you are ready, you will work unsupervised and be fully operational.

Custodial Care NVQ (CCNVQ) Level 3

As a new Prison Officer you will be required to complete a CCNVQ within your probationary period. This will give you the satisfaction of a formal qualification as well as increasing your confidence to carry out your role effectively.

WHAT IS IT LIKE WORKING AS A PRISON OFFICER?

Steve is 42 years old and is married with one daughter aged

15 and one son aged 17. He is a Prison Officer in a male, category C/B prison and has been in the role for over 5 years now. When Steve left school he worked as an engineer in the Armed Forces but after a while this role became stale to him and he decided that he wanted a new challenge. He noticed an advertisement in a local newspaper placed by the Prison Service, who were recruiting Prison Officers in his area. As soon as he saw the advert he knew that this was what he wanted to do. The job security and working in a close-knit team were the two most important areas that appealed to him. He was required to sit an entrance test, which consisted of Mathematics, English and a speed test in numeracy. He was then assessed on his reactions to a number of different scenarios, one of which was a man who screamed and shouted at him as soon as he walked into the assessment room! This was followed by a medical and fitness test, which involved a number of areas including the bleep test.

Steve passed all of the tests but had to wait 6 months until a vacancy arose. He completed 8 weeks' training followed by a 12-month probationary period. He is now working on a wing that houses 130 prisoners, 110 of whom have a job or are on an educational course within the prison. (If they don't do either of these, they have to stay locked up.) He says it's a brilliant job where no 2 days are the same and he would recommend it to anyone!

A LOOK INSIDE A PRISON

Gatehouse

This is the area where staff check the identification of all visitors, staff and prisoners when they arrive. Contractors who work within the prison will also be verified here. You will find that there is a strict booking in/out process too.

Reception

All prisoners that come to or leave the prison are searched within the reception area. You will sometimes find that the reception forms an integral part of the Gatehouse.

Health Care Centre

Healthcare centres are predominantly used to check the welfare and health of prisoners. Prisoners are able to visit the nurse, dentist and optician here if and when required to do so.

Gymnasium

This is the area where prisoners perform some of their exercise under supervision. Some prisons also have football/recreation pitches within their grounds. Sport and recreation forms an integral part of a prisoner's rehabilitation.

Accommodation

Prisoners live in accommodation blocks, which are either cellular in design or dormitory style. Within the accommodation blocks are washing/showering facilities, food serving areas, TV areas and telephones. The facilities available will vary greatly from prison to prison.

Recreation Area

The recreation area is usually an open space where prisoners can mix together, sometimes watch television or play games such as cards, board games or pool if available. Some recreation areas form part of the accommodation blocks. Again, each prison will vary dependant upon category and design etc.

Visitors Centre

This is the area where prisoners' friends, families and relatives can visit them. A convicted prisoner must apply for

a visiting order prior to any visit. This area may also have facilities where prisoners and their visitors can purchase drinks and snacks etc. Again, each prison will vary but pre-checks are also carried out in these areas to check the identity of visitors.

Chaplaincy

Most prisons will employ an Anglican Chaplain on a full time basis to care for prisoners and also staff when required. Members of the chaplaincy team need to be able to cater for specific religious faiths including Roman Catholic, Hindu, Jewish and Muslim etc. Some Prison Chaplaincies will operate on a part-time basis dependant upon the number of prisoners etc.

Education Centre

Prison establishments have to work towards Key Performance Targets (KPTs) in terms of prisoner education. The education centre provides facilities for prisoners who need to learn basic skills or for those who want to work towards GCSEs or A-Levels etc.

CHAPTER 2
THE PRISON OFFICER SELECTION PROCESS

The Prison Service is very careful about the way in which they process applications for the role of Prison Officer. As you can imagine, it takes a special kind of person to be able to deal effectively with the situations that a Prison Officer will find him/herself in on a daily basis. The selection process is designed to assess whether or not you have the right qualities to carry out the role competently. Below you will see an outline of how the selection process works.

RECEIPT OF APPLICATIONS

You can usually apply to become a prison officer online via the website www.hmprisonservice.gov.uk. From this website you can also search for Prison Officer jobs in your preferred area. The Prison Service will sometimes use the website www.whatsontheinside.co.uk as their main recruitment portal.

If you meet the minimum eligibility requirements, your application will be acknowledged by email as soon as you submit it. You will then be invited to sit an online version of the Prison Officer Selection Test, which is more commonly referred to as the POST.

PRISON OFFICER SELECTION TEST (POST) – online version

Once your application has been accepted you will be sent a link via email to take an electronic online version of the Prison Officer Selection Test (POST). This stage of the POST consists of numerical tests, comprising of a number of work sample exercises. You won't, however, require any prior knowledge of prison work in order to undertake the test.

Within a later section of this guide I have provided you with plenty of sample test questions to help you prepare for the POST.

If successful at the online POST stage, you will then be invited to attend the Recruitment Assessment Day (RAD).

RECRUITMENT ASSESSMENT DAY (RAD)

The Recruitment Assessment Day has been designed to test several elements that are needed in the Prison Officer role - these include;

- 4 role-play simulations, each lasting a maximum of ten minutes.

The scenarios that you will encounter during the role-plays are usually non-prison based. However they are similar to situations you could face as a Prison Officer.

POST NUMERACY TEST

As part of the Recruitment Assessment Day you will also be required to complete a shorter paper-based version of the online POST that you previously sat.

POST LANGUAGE TEST

The second element of your Recruitment Assessment Day Prison Officer Selection Test is a paper-based language test, which includes some observational skills questions that assess the following key areas:

- Completing forms and reading information;

- Checking information for errors and discrepancies;

- Carrying out written observations of seen information.

THE FITNESS TEST

Candidates are normally required to take the fitness test during the Recruitment Assessment Day. The test itself is designed to assess some elements of a Prison Officer's role and consists of the following assessable areas:

- Grip strength test;

- Multi-stage fitness test (often called the bleep test);

- Dynamic strength test;

- Speed agility run test;

- Shield test.

During a later section of the guide I have provided you with a free 'How to get Prison Officer fit' information guide. The exercises that I have provided you with will go a long way to

helping you pass the fitness test element of the Recruitment Assessment Day.

MEDICAL AND VETTING

Following the successful completion of all previous elements of the selection process, you will then undertake a medical and vetting checks. The medical will assess your overall health and fitness for becoming a Prison Officer. The vetting checks are standard procedure and include identity checks, nationality and character checks and a criminal record check. These checks can take up to 8 weeks to complete so you will need to be patient.

Once you have passed every element of the selection process you will normally be offered an appointment and starting date. However, in some circumstances you will be placed on a reserve list, which has a validity of 18 months. As soon as a vacancy becomes available you will be offered a place.

CHAPTER 3
THE TOP 10 TIPS AND ADVICE

Within this section of the guide I will provide you with 10 very important tips that will help you to successfully pass the Prison Officer selection process. Some of the tips may appear to be obvious, but you would be surprised how many people fail to focus on them during their preparation. Follow and implement each one of them carefully and your chances of success will increase dramatically.

TIP I
Have a thorough understanding of the selection process
Many people fail the initial stages of the selection process through a general lack of preparation. It is important to put yourself in the shoes of the people who will be assessing you. What are they looking for in a successful candidate? Once you have the answer to this question you will then be able formulate an action plan that will lead you to success. Having spent time speaking to serving Prison Officers and

recruitment staff, the follow areas are ones that you must focus on:

Numerical competence

How good are you with numbers? Can you carry out basic numerical calculations such as addition, subtraction, multiplication, division, ratios, percentages etc? Part of the role of a Prison Officer requires you carry out these and other numerical calculations. Therefore, during the selection process you will be assessed against your numerical competence, both during the online POST and also at the Recruitment Assessment Day. Make sure you carry out plenty of practice in this area prior to the tests. I have provided lots of sample questions to help you prepare during a later section of this guide.

The six core behavioural skills

The core behavioural skills are essential to the role of a Prison Officer. They are effectively the foundations of the role, and without them, Prison Officers would not be able to carry out the job as professionally as they do. The core behavioural skills are non-verbal communication, showing understanding, suspending judgement, assertion, respect for diversity and exploring and clarifying. I have dedicated an entire section to these important skills later on within the guide. If you are to have any chance of successfully passing the role-play scenarios that form part of the Recruitment Assessment Day then you must learn to demonstrate each and every one of these!

Physical fitness

Whilst you do not need to be as fit as an Olympic athlete in order to become a Prison Officer, you do need to have a 'better than average' level of fitness. The role requires you to carry out Control and Restraint (C & R) procedures and

you may also have to run/sprint at certain times during your career. Therefore, the recruitment officers want to know that you are capable of carrying out your tasks and duties without collapsing due to a lack of physical fitness. The current standard used to assess your fitness levels is as follows:

- Grip strength test

- Multi-stage fitness test

- Dynamic strength test

- Speed agility run test

- Shield Test

Towards the end of this guide I have provided you with a 'How to get Prison Officer fit' information guide, which contains lots of exercises that will help you to pass this stage of selection.

Whilst there are other areas you will need to concentrate on during your preparation, I strongly advise that you primarily work on the above. Concentrate on the above three areas and the information contained within this guide and you will achieve greater scores during the Prison Officer Selection Test and the Recruitment Assessment Day.

TIP 2
Read the prison service Statement of Purpose
Just like any other public service, the Prison Service must lay down its aims and objectives. Sometimes this is called a 'mission statement' or 'aims and objectives'. The Prison Service's 'Statement of Purpose' states what they are aiming to achieve in terms of standards. It is worth reading and absorbing the statement because it will give you an understanding of what the Prison Service expects from its staff, including Prison Officers.

The Statement of Purpose details their vision, principles and objectives and I advise you learn it so as to improve your knowledge of the service you are applying to join. Whilst you will not normally be assessed against it, it will serve to widen your knowledge in relation to the job you are applying for. At the time of writing the Prison Service statement is as follows:

Statement of Purpose

Her Majesty's Prison Service serves the public by keeping in custody those committed by the courts. Our duty is to look after them with humanity and help them lead law-abiding and useful lives in custody and after release.

Our Vision

- To provide the very best prison services so that we are the provider of choice

- To work towards this vision by securing the following key objectives.

Objectives

To protect the public and provide what commissioners want to purchase by:

- Holding prisoners securely

- Reducing the risk of prisoners re-offending

- Providing safe and well-ordered establishments in which we treat prisoners humanely, decently and lawfully.

In securing these objectives we adhere to the following principles:

Our Principles

In carrying out our work we:

- Work in close partnership with our commissioners and others in the Criminal Justice System to achieve common objectives

- Obtain best value from the resources available using research to ensure effective correctional practice

- Promote diversity, equality of opportunity and combat unlawful discrimination, and

- Ensure our staff have the right leadership, organisation, support and preparation to carry out their work effectively.

Crown copyright © 2004

You will notice that the Statement of Purpose mentions that it is the duty of the Prison Service to look after convicted prisoners with humanity and help them to lead law-abiding and useful lives in custody and after release. There is no room for bullying or harassment within the Prison Service and you must be prepared to act in a manner that is consistent with this important statement.

TIP 3

Work on your reading and observational skills

During the Recruitment Assessment Day you will be required to sit a Language Test. Part of the test involves the following:

Reading comprehension You will read text extracted from a standard Prison Service source (e.g. Prison Service Orders, intranet, manuals etc) and then answer questions about the text.

In order to successfully pass the above test, you will need to be able to read extracted information carefully so that you can answer questions based on the information provided.

There is only one way to improve your reading skills, and that is to actually read extracts of information. Sit down and read an article of interest from your favourite newspaper or alternatively read a number of Prison Service Orders, which can be found here:

www.prisonserviceorders.co.uk

Reading and familiarising yourself with Prison Service Orders will also be great preparation for the role.

TIP 4
Have respect for diversity at all times

In today's society it is important that we have respect for diversity and this applies to the role of the Prison Officer too. In basic terms, diversity can be defined as follows:

> The concept of diversity encompasses acceptance and respect.
>
> It means understanding that each individual is unique, and recognising our individual differences. These can be along the dimensions of race, ethnicity, gender, sexual orientation, socio-economic status, age, physical abilities, religious beliefs, political beliefs, or other ideologies. It is the exploration of these differences in a safe, positive, and nurturing environment. It is about understanding each other and moving beyond simple tolerance to embracing and celebrating the rich dimensions of diversity contained within each individual.

The concept of diversity encompasses acceptance and respect.

It means understanding that each individual is unique, and recognising our individual differences. These can be along the dimensions of race, ethnicity, gender, sexual orientation, socio-economic status, age, physical abilities, religious beliefs, political beliefs, or other ideologies. It is the exploration of these differences in a safe, positive, and nurturing environment. It is about understanding each other and moving beyond simple tolerance to embracing and celebrating the rich dimensions of diversity contained within each individual.

As a Prison Officer you will be supporting and looking after people from diverse backgrounds who will often have opinions and views that are different to your own. In addition to this you will also have to work with people from diverse backgrounds. Part of the Prison Service's Statement of Purpose makes a commitment towards valuing diversity, promoting equality of opportunity and combating unlawful discrimination.

As a Prison Officer you will need to believe in, and promote these important values. As part of the Recruitment Assessment Day role-play scenarios you will be required to demonstrate respect for diversity. Whilst I will explain more about the importance of diversity later on during the 'core behavioural skills' section of the guide, there are ways to improve your knowledge and understanding in this area. One way is to visit the Commission for Racial Equality website, which can be found at www.equalityhumanrights.com.

TIP 5
Understand the difference between assertion and agression
You will recall that one of the 6 core behavioural skills is that of 'assertion'. As a Prison Officer you will need to use this skill just about every day that you are on duty. There is a

fine line, however, between assertion and aggression, and it is essential that you do not cross it. You will be assessed against your ability to be assertive during the role-play scenarios that form part of the Recruitment Assessment Day.

Assertive behaviour is that where a person is able to positively state with assurance, confidence or force, his/her own belief or position. As a Prison Officer you will usually demonstrate assertion in relation to rules or regulations. For example, if a prisoner is refusing to go back to his or her accommodation then you will need to demonstrate a level of assertion because the prisoner is acting outside of Prison Service rules.

The problem comes for many people when they try to demonstrate assertion, but they start to show signs of aggression. You can be assertive and achieve a positive outcome by talking calmly. You do not normally have to shout or show aggressive body language in order to assert your position. In fact, by simply doing and saying nothing you can more often than not take the sting out of a potentially confrontational situation and achieve the desired outcome.

Ways to demonstrate assertive behaviour during the role-play scenarios

- Standing firm in a non-confrontation manner. Crossing your arms or showing an angry face is more likely to enflame a situation.

- Speaking with a raised voice but never shouting.

- Not being persuaded to change your position or decision.

- Being firm in the manner in which you communicate.

I will provide further advice and information on how to

demonstrate assertiveness during a later section of this guide. However, the key point here is to make sure that you never become aggressive during the role-play scenarios, regardless of how the role actor is being towards you!

TIP 6
Don't jump to conclusions!

One of the great qualities of a Prison Officer is the ability to explore and clarify before making judgements about people and situations. If you are to become a competent Prison Officer then you too will need to learn the important skill of 'suspending judgement'.

As part of the Recruitment Assessment Day you will be assessed against this behavioural skill during the role-play scenarios. Suspending judgement effectively means not making any inappropriate interruptions and suspending your judgements on what you are hearing in the role-play simulation before deciding on the right course of action to take. Suspending judgement is relatively simple to demonstrate. All you need to do is enter the role-play scenario and listen carefully to what is being said by the role-play actor. You would normally not interrupt them, unless inappropriate language was being used, and you would explore and clarify by asking them appropriate questions. You will often find that things aren't quite as they seem on first appearances!

TIP 7
Use an action plan to ensure success

An action plan will focus your mind on the task that lies ahead of you. If I were applying to become a Prison Officer today then I would most probably use a weekly timetable of preparation that looks something like this:

Monday	Tuesday	Wednesday	Thursday	Friday	Saturday	Sunday
45 minutes researching the role of a Prison Officer and the Prison Service.	60 minutes study in relation to the Prison Officer Selection Test (POST).	Spend 60 minutes learning the six core behavioural skills.	Rest day	45 minutes researching the role of a Prison Officer and the Prison Service.	60 minutes study in relation to the Prison Officer Selection Test (POST).	60 minutes trying out some mock role-play scenarios with a friend or relative.
30-minute run or brisk walk	45 minutes gym work (light weights).	30-minute run or bleep test preparation.	3-mile run (best effort) and bleep test preparation.	60 minutes preparation for the Prison Officer Selection Test (POST).	45 minutes gym work (light weights) or 30-minute swim.	

The above timetable would ensure that I focused on the following three key development areas:

1. Improving my ability to pass the Prison Officer Selection Test (POST);

2. Improving my physical fitness in preparation for the physical tests.

3. Improving my knowledge of the Prison Service and the role of a Prison Officer.

The point I am trying to get across here is that if you add some form of 'structure' to your preparation then you are far more likely to succeed. Following a structured training and development programme during your preparation for selection will increase your chances of success greatly.

TIP 8
Work on improving your fitness by using 'targeted' exercise and workouts
Make sure that you are both physically and mentally fit.

You certainly don't need to be into bodybuilding or as fit as an Olympic runner to become a Prison Officer. Yes, it is true that you have to meet a certain level of fitness to pass the physical tests but if you prepare well in advance you can become fit enough with a few easy steps.

During your preparation it may be worth considering changing your diet to make sure that you are eating the correct foods. Make sure you eat foods that will give you energy and also those that contain the right vitamins to ensure you are at your best. If you think you are overweight then the best form of exercise to take in order to lose weight is walking at a brisk pace every day for at least 20 minutes. You'll be amazed at the difference you feel in just a few weeks. Then you can progress onto jogging and light gym work.

In relation to your mental fitness, cut out alcohol and caffeine in the weeks leading up to your Recruitment Assessment Day. Drink plenty of water and try to eat your five portions of fruit and vegetables every day. Again, you will be amazed at how much energy you gain simply by looking after yourself.

Depending on your current level of fitness, I would advise that you spend approximately 25% of your total preparation time on improving your fitness levels.

Action points

- Embark on a structured fitness programme that is designed to help you pass the physical tests. See the Prison Officer fitness guide section for some useful tips and advice.

- Drink plenty of water during your preparation.

- Cut out alcohol and caffeine during your preparation.

- Eat healthily.

TIP 9

Be competent in the use of the 24-hour clock

Jobs of this nature require you to be competent in the use of the 24-hour clock. During the Prison Officer Selection Test (POST) you will be required to answer a number of questions that are based around the use of the 24-hour clock. There are effectively two ways to show the time: "AM/PM" or "24-hour clock":

- With the 24-Hour Clock the time is shown as how many hours and minutes have passed since midnight.

- With AM/PM (or the "12-Hour Clock") the day is split into the 12 hours running from midnight to noon (the AM hours) and the other 12 hours running from noon to midnight (the PM hours).

Converting AM/PM to 24-hour clock

For the first hour of the day (12 midnight to 12:59 AM), subtract 12 hours.

Examples:
12 midnight = 0:00, 12:35 AM = 0:35
From 1:00 AM to 12:59 PM, no change

Examples:
11:20 AM = 11:20, 12:30 PM = 12:30
From 1:00 PM to 11:59 PM, add 12 hours

Examples:
4:45 PM = 16:45, 11:50 PM = 23:50

Converting 24-hour clock to AM/PM

For the first hour of the day (0:00 to 0:59), add 12 hours, make it "AM"

Examples:
0:10 = 12:10 AM, 0:40 = 12:40 AM
From 1:00 to 11:59, just make it "AM"

Examples:
1:15 = 1:15 AM, 11:25 = 11:25 AM
From 12:00 to 12:59, just make it "PM"

Examples:
12:10 = 12:10 PM, 12:55 = 12:55 PM
From 13:00 to 23:59, subtract 12 hours and make it "PM"

Examples:
14:55 = 2:55 PM, 23:30 = 11:30 PM

Conversion chart

Here is a side-by-side comparison of the 24-hour clock and AM/PM:

0:00	12:00 Midnight		12:00	12:00 Noon
01:00	1:00 AM		13:00	1:00 PM
02:00	2:00 AM		14:00	2:00 PM
03:00	3:00 AM		15:00	3:00 PM
04:00	4:00 AM		16:00	4:00 PM
05:00	5:00 AM		17:00	5:00 PM
06:00	6:00 AM		18:00	6:00 PM
07:00	7:00 AM		19:00	7:00 PM
08:00	8:00 AM		20:00	8:00 PM
09:00	9:00 AM		21:00	9:00 PM
10:00	10:00 AM		22:00	10:00 PM
11:00	11:00 AM		23:00	11:00 PM

Before you sit the online version of the Prison Officer Selection Test, make sure you are competent in the use of the 24-hour clock.

TIP 10

Attention to detail!

As a Prison Officer you will be responsible for checking information for errors and discrepancies. Therefore, your ability to spot mistakes is crucial. During the role you will be required to crosscheck prisoners with cell locations and make sure people are where they are supposed to be. If somebody is missing, then you need to spot it quickly.

During the Recruitment Assessment Day you will sit a language test. This test assesses you against:

- **Listening, taking notes and recalling heard information** – You will listen to an oral briefing about events in a prison. You will be advised to take notes on rough paper provided. On completion of the briefing you will be asked to write down answers to questions relating to the information you have just heard.

- **Completing a standard form** – You will complete a standard form using written information provided about a prisoner.

- **Checking information for discrepancies, errors and omissions** – You will compare two lists and identify discrepancies and/or omissions on the second list.

- **Applying rules** – You will be presented with two lists; the first shows cells where prisoners belong (sleep) on a prison wing; the second shows where they are currently located on the wing. You will compare the information on these two lists, and apply three rules in order to determine if everyone is present on the wing and who (if anyone) is breaking the rules.

- **Reading comprehension** – You will read text extracted from a standard Prison Service source (e.g. Prison

Service Orders, intranet, manuals etc) and then answer questions about the text.

- **Recalling visual (seen) information from memory** – You will be shown a colour photograph of a prison scene for three minutes. The photograph is removed and you will be asked several questions about what you saw. Note taking is not permitted on this exercise.

As you can see from the test, there is a strong emphasis on attention to detail. You are required to listen to information, read text, compare lists, check for discrepancies and recall information.

Your ability to apply attention to detail during this part of the assessment is very important.

CHAPTER 4
THE PRISON OFFICER SELECTION TEST (POST)

Once you have made your initial online application, and it has been successful, you will be invited to sit an online Prison Officer Selection Test (POST). The test itself is designed to be representative of the types of numerical tasks that Prison Officers are required to carry out on a daily basis.

There are four sections to the test consisting of a total of 56 questions. You have 60 minutes to complete the test, which equates to approximately 15 minutes per section. It is very important that you are the person who actually carries out the test, as there is a similar version of the POST to be undertaken at the Recruitment Assessment Day.

The good news is you are permitted to use a calculator and you do not lose any marks for incorrect answers. The questions that you will face during the online POST are pre-dominantly based around numerical reasoning and include:

- Addition, subtraction, multiplication and division;

- The use of the 24-hour clock;

- Ratios and percentages;

- Cross referencing lists and checking information.

- Interpreting graphs and charts.

Once you have successfully passed the online POST you will be invited to attend a Recruitment Assessment Day. During the Recruitment Assessment Day you will sit a language test. This test assesses you against:

- **Listening, taking notes and recalling heard information** – You will listen to an oral briefing about events in a prison. You will be advised to take notes on rough paper provided. On completion of the briefing you will be asked to write down answers to questions relating to the information you have just heard.

- **Completing a standard form** – You will complete a standard form using written information provided about a prisoner.

- **Checking information for discrepancies, errors and omissions** – You will compare two lists and identify discrepancies and/or omissions on the second list.

- **Applying rules** – You will be presented with two lists; the first shows cells where prisoners belong (sleep) on a prison wing; the second shows where they are currently located on the wing. You will compare the information on these two lists, and apply three rules in order to determine if everyone is present on the wing and who (if anyone) is breaking the rules.

- **Reading comprehension** – You will read text extracted

from a standard Prison Service source (e.g. Prison Service Orders, intranet, manuals etc) and then answer questions about the text.

• **Recalling visual (seen) information from memory** – You will be shown a colour photograph of a prison scene for three minutes. The photograph is removed and you will be asked several questions about what you saw. Note taking is not permitted on this exercise.

Over the next few chapters I have provided you with four sample tests that will go a long way to helping you prepare effectively. The questions contained within the tests are similar to the types you will encounter during the online POST and also the POST at the Recruitment Assessment Day.

Once you have completed each test, take the time to check your answers thoroughly.

CHAPTER 5
SAMPLE PRISON OFFICER SELECTION TEST (POST) NUMBER I

During sample POST number 1 there are 40 questions. You have 20 minutes to complete the test. You are permitted to use a calculator.

The following diagram represents prisoners serving at HMP Fictown and their different locations.

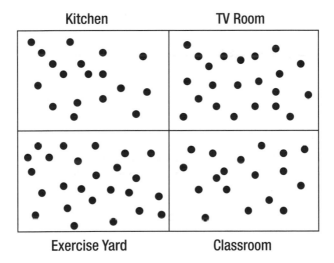

Key: ● = 1 prisoner

Question 1

How many prisoners are there in the Classroom?

Answer

Question 2

How many prisoners are there in the Exercise yard?

Answer

Question 3

How many prisoners are there in the Kitchen?

Answer

Question 4

How many prisoners are there in total?

Answer

Question 5

If 50% of prisoners in the Kitchen move to the TV room, how many prisoners will be left in the Kitchen?

Answer

Question 6

If 50% of prisoners in the TV room move to the Exercise yard, how many prisoners will there now be in the Exercise yard?

Answer

Question 7

If 20% of prisoners leave the Exercise yard, how many prisoners will there now be left in the Exercise yard?

Answer

The following diagram represents prisoners serving at HMP Spillfield and their different locations.

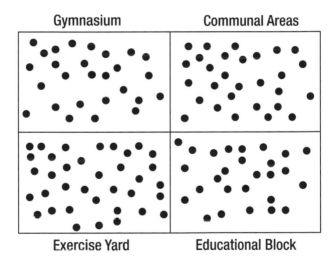

Key: ● = 1 prisoner

Question 8

How many prisoners are there in total?

Answer [   ]

Question 9

How many prisoners are there in the Gymnasium and the Educational block combined?

Answer [   ]

Question 10

How many prisoners are there in Exercise yard and the Communal areas combined?

Answer [   ]

Question 11

If 50% of prisoners in the Exercise yard move to the Gymnasium, how many prisoners will there now be in the Gymnasium?

Answer [   ]

Question 12

If 25% of prisoners in the Exercise yard move to the Educational block, how many prisoners will there now be in the Exercise yard?

Answer

The following diagram represents prisoners serving at HMP Frintern and their different locations.

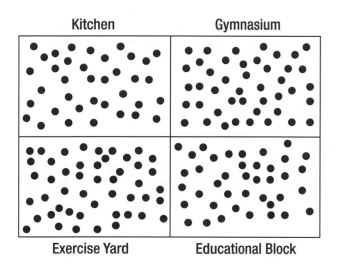

Key: ● = 1 prisoner

Question 13

How many prisoners are there in total?

Answer

Question 14

If 5% of prisoners move from the Educational block to the Kitchen, how many prisoners will there now be in the

Kitchen?

Answer

Question 15

If 40% of prisoners move from the Educational block to the Gymnasium, how many prisoners will there now be in the Educational block?

Answer

Question 16

If 25% of prisoners move from the Gymnasium to the Exercise yard, how many prisoners will there now be in the Gymnasium?

Answer

Question 17

How many prisoners are there in the Gymnasium, Exercise yard and the Kitchen combined?

Answer

Question 18

If 50% of prisoners in the Gymnasium and 50% of prisoners in the Educational block all move to the Kitchen, how many prisoners would there now be in the Kitchen?

Answer

Question 19

If 50% of prisoners in the Exercise yard, 25% of prisoners in the Educational block, and 50% of prisoners in the Gymnasium all move to the Kitchen, how many prisoners would there now be in the Kitchen?

Answer [   ]

The following diagram represents prisoners serving at HMP Merrydown and their different locations.

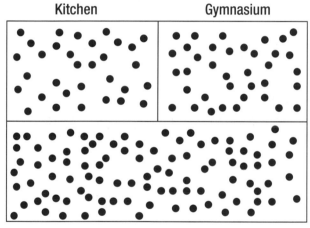

Key: ● = 1 prisoner

Question 20

How many prisoners are there in total?

Answer

Question 21

How many prisoners are there in the Communal areas and the Gymnasium combined total?

Answer

Question 22

If 50% of prisoners in the Kitchen move to the Communal areas, how many prisoners are there now in the Communal areas?

Answer

Question 23

If 75% of prisoners in the Communal areas move to the Gymnasium, how many prisoners will there now be in the Gymnasium?

Answer

Question 24

If 75% of prisoners in the Communal areas move to the Gymnasium, how many prisoners will there now be in the Communal areas?

Answer

Question 25

If 25% of prisoners in the Kitchen move to the Gymnasium, and 50% of prisoners in the Communal areas move to the Gymnasium, how many prisoners will there be now in the Gymnasium

Answer [   ]

Question 26

In total there are 150 prisoners living on a wing of a prison and there are 15 prison officers on duty. What is the ratio of prisoners to prison officers?

Answer [   ]

Question 27

In total there are 120 prisoners living on a wing of a prison and there are 6 prison officers on duty. What is the ratio of prisoners to prison officers?

Answer [   ]

Question 28

In total there are 220 prisoners living on a wing of a prison and there are 10 prison officers on duty. What is the ratio of prisoners to prison officers?

Answer [   ]

Question 29

In total there are 320 prisoners at HMP Pickleberry and there are 40 prison officers on duty. What is the ratio of prisoners to prison officers?

Answer

Question 30

In total there are 320 prisoners at HMP Pickleberry and there are 4 female prison officers on duty. What is the ratio of prisoners to female prison officers?

Answer

Question 31

At HMP Pickleberry there are a total of 40 prison officers, of which 36 are male and 4 are female. What is the ratio of male prison officers to female prison officers?

Answer

Question 32

At HMP Pickleberry there are a total of 320 prisoners, of which 110 are category A prisoners, 98 are category B prisoners and the remainder are category C prisoners. How many prisoners are category C?

Answer

Question 33

At HMP Wardale there are a total of 400 prisoners, of

which 56 are category A prisoners, 44 are category B prisoners and the remainder are category C prisoners. What percentage of the total number of prisoners at HMP Wardale is category C?

Answer

Question 34

92 prisoners live on Blue Wing. Of these, 28 have gone to the educational centre, 17 have gone to the music group and 6 have gone to see the nurse. How many prisoners remain on Blue wing?

Answer

Question 35

99 prisoners live on Purple Wing. Of these, 15 have gone to the educational centre, 12 have gone to the music group and 4 have gone to see the nurse. How many prisoners remain on Purple wing?

Answer

Question 36

87 prisoners live on Red Wing. Of these, 22 have gone to the TV room, 13 have gone to see the nurse and 41 have gone to the exercise yard. How many prisoners remain on Red wing?

Answer

Question 37

91 prisoners live on Yellow Wing. Of these, 1 has gone to see the nurse, 17 have gone to work in the laundry, 18 have gone to the shower area, 5 have gone to the classroom and the remainder have gone to the gymnasium. How many have gone to the gymnasium?

Answer

Question 38

110 prisoners live on Green Wing. Of these, 10% have gone to see the nurse, 20% have gone to the educational block, 50% have gone to the exercise yard and 20% have stayed on the wing. How many prisoners have stayed on the wing?

Answer

Question 39

114 prisoners live on D Wing, which is currently fully occupied. There are 2 beds occupying each cell. How many cells are there on D Wing?

Answer

Question 40

987 prisoners occupy the prison. Of these:

- 134 have gone to the gymnasium
- 161 have gone to visit the health centre
- 19 are in the workshop

- 11 have gone to the education centre
- 40 are in the dining area
- 231 are in the visitors centre

The remaining prisoners are in their cells.

How many prisoners are in their cells?

Answer

ANSWERS TO SAMPLE PRISON OFFICER SELECTION TEST (POST) NUMBER 1

1.	18	**11.**	45	**21.**	133	**31.**	9:1
2.	25	**12.**	27	**22.**	112	**32.**	112
3.	18	**13.**	169	**23.**	109	**33.**	75%
4.	83	**14.**	39	**24.**	24	**34.**	41
5.	9	**15.**	24	**25.**	93	**35.**	68
6.	36	**16.**	33	**26.**	10:1	**36.**	11
7.	20	**17.**	129	**27.**	20:1	**37.**	50
8.	119	**18.**	79	**28.**	22:1	**38.**	22
9.	54	**19.**	93	**29.**	8:1	**39.**	57
10.	65	**20.**	165	**30.**	80:1	**40.**	391

how2become

CHAPTER 6
SAMPLE PRISON OFFICER SELECTION TEST (POST) NUMBER 2

During sample POST number 2 there are 40 questions. You have 20 minutes to complete the test. You are permitted to use a calculator.

Question 1

At HMP Smithstreet prisoners earn 60p a day for working in the workshop. How much does a prisoner earn for 5 days work?

Answer

Question 2

You are supervising a number of prisoners who are working out in the gymnasium. Two prisoners are using the rowing

machines, five are carrying out press-ups, two are using the running machines and seven are resting. How many prisoners are carrying out exercises?

Answer

Question 3

Prison officers are required to use the 24-hour clock (e.g. 3.45pm = 15.45). Convert the following times to the 24-hour clock.

a) 7.07 pm
b) 6.35 pm

Answer

Question 4

Compare the following two lists below. Write down the number of the line(s) where you identify a difference between the two lists.

1.	Car	33	Blue	Cat	Chicken
2.	Ban	33	Blue	Fish	Meat
3.	Lorry	2123	Yellow	Horse	Dairy
4.	Plane	6	Pink	House	Fat
5.	Sail	191	Black	Chair	Noodle
6.	Ball	300	Brown	Mouse	Rice
7.	Hall	456	Orange	Mice	Egg
8.	Bridge	210	Grey	Shark	Banana
9.	Road	876	Green	Hippo	Bread
10.	Sea	65	Blue	Stair	Food

1.	Car	33	Blue	Cat	Chicken
2.	Van	33	Blue	Fish	Meat
3.	Lorry	2123	Yellow	Horse	Dairy
4.	Plane	6	Pink	Garage	Fat
5.	Sail	191	Black	Chair	Noodle
6.	Ball	300	Brown	Mouse	Rice
7.	Hall	456	Orange	Mice	Egg
8.	Bridge	21	Grey	Shark	Banana
9.	Road	876	Green	Hippo	Bread
10.	Sea	65	Blue	Stair	Food

You have been assigned to 'A' Wing at your first prison. List A is the official location of your prisoners. Prisoners can move freely around A wing providing they adhere to the following rules:

RULES:

1. Prisoners in cells D2, D4 and D5 are not allowed in cells A1, A2 and A3.

2. No more than 3 prisoners are allowed in one cell at any one time.

Your supervisory manager has asked you to check the locations of all your prisoners to ensure none of them is breaking the rules.

List A: Official cell locations

A1 Gardner, Macintosh	**D1** Craig, Barton, Mitchell
A2 Eubank, Gregson	**D2** Emery, Davis
A3 Hardy, Coombs	**D3** Matcham

A4 Welsh, Davies, Wallis	**D4** Savage, Taylor
A5 Benny, Norris, Carter	**D5** Armstrong, Fridd

List B is the observations you find after your investigation.

List B: Your observations

A1 Gardner, Armstrong, Mitchell	**D1** Craig, Barton, Mitchell
A2 Eubank, Gregson, Savage	**D2** Emery, Davis, Fridd
A3 Hardy, Coombs, Matcham	**D3**
A4 Welsh, Wallis	**D4** Taylor
A5 Benny, Norris, Carter	**D5**

Question 5

Is anybody missing? If so, who?

Answer

Question 6

Who is contravening Rule 1?

Answer

Question 7

Who is contravening Rule 2?

Answer

Question 8

Compare the following two lists below. Write down the number of the line(s) where you identify a difference between the two lists.

1.	Yellow	9349	Pink	Humour	Dating
2.	Peach	23wErt	Bill	90816	Fair
3.	Yasmin	Part	Ball	Tree	Fern
4.	871654	8	815643	Train	Cat
5.	Cow	220847	Burden	Difficult	Club
6.	13242627	80165	671yUtr	Bg14321	9065Rt
7.	Grl1432	Yupp7D	Me3Er41	871Yt	Jug1
8.	Debt	Pardon	Plush	peanut	Noodle
9.	Clever	891uy	Orange	snooze	Very
10.	Piglet	Dim	7265	Moon	Kite

1.	Yellow	9349	Blink	Humour	Dating
2.	Beach	23wErt	Bill	90816	Fern
3.	Yasmin	Part	Ball	Tree	Dairy
4.	871654	8	815643	Train	Cat
5.	Cow	220847	Burden	Difficult	Club
6.	13242627	80165	671yUtr	Bg14321	9065Rt
7.	Grl1432	Yup7D	Me3Er41	871Yt	Jug1
8.	Debt	pardon	Plush	Peanut	Noodle
9.	Clever	891uy	Orange	snooze	Very
10.	Piglet	Dim	71265	Moon	Kite

The following diagram represents prisoners serving at HMP Bunting and their different locations.

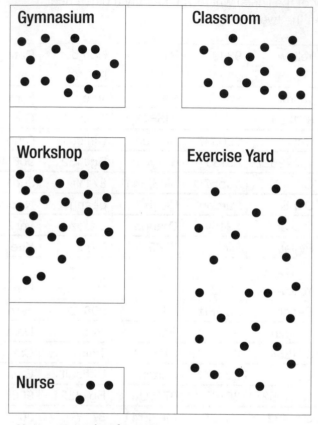

Key: ● = 1 prisoner

Question 9

How many prisoners are there in total at HMP Bunting?

Answer [   ]

Question 10

If 50% of prisoners in the exercise yard move to the workshop, how many prisoners will there now be in the workshop?

Answer [   ]

Question 11

If 4 prisoners from the gymnasium, 2 prisoners from the classroom and 2 prisoners who are seeing the nurse all move to the exercise yard, how many prisoners will there now be in the exercise yard?

Answer [   ]

Question 12

If 50% of prisoners in the workshop and 25% of prisoners in the exercise yard all move to the classroom, how many prisoners will there now be in the classroom?

Answer [   ]

Question 13

If there are 13 prison officers on duty at HMP Bunting, what is the ratio of prisoners to prison officers?

Answer [   ]

Question 14

Out of the total number of prisoners at HMP Bunting, 6 are category A. How many prisoners are not category A?

Answer

Question 15

If a third of prisoners leave HMP Bunting, how many prisoners remain?

Answer

Question 16

460 people apply to become a prison officer. Of this number, 60% are male and 40% are female. How many female applicants are there?

Answer

Question 17

290 people apply to become a prison officer. Of this number, 70% are male and 30% are female. How many male applicants are there?

Answer

HMP Stumbling has 445 prisoners; the sentence breakdown is as follows:

Wing	Length of Sentence	
	Long term	Short term
Blue	90	10
Red	80	15
Purple	60	20
White	75	5
Green	60	30

Question 18

How many short-term prisoners are there in total?

Answer

Question 19

How many long-term prisoners are there in total?

Answer

Question 20

All short-term prisoners on wings green, white and red are transferred to another prison. How many prisoners remain at HMP Stumbling?

Answer

Question 21

50% of long-term prisoners on wings red and green are transferred to another prison. How many prisoners remain at HMP Stumbling?

Answer [   ]

Question 22

70 prison officers work at HMP Stumbling. Of these:

20 work on Blue wing;
20 work on Red wing;
10 work on White wing;

Of the remaining prison officers 25% work on Green wing and 75% work on Purple wing. How many prison officers work on Purple wing?

Answer [   ]

HMP Garton has 290 prisoners; the sentence breakdown is as follows:

Wing	Length of Sentence	
	Long term	Short term
Yellow	60	10
Brown	45	15
Blue	75	20
White	35	5
Green	20	5

Question 23

If the ratio of prisoners to prison officers at HMP Garton is 10:1, how many prison officers are there?

Answer

Question 24

If 30% of long-term prisoners on Yellow wing, 25% of long-term prisoners on Green wing, and 75% of short-term prisoners on Blue wing leave the prison, how many prisoners will there be now at HMP Garton?

Answer

Question 25

If 20% of long-term prisoners and 20% of short-term prisoners are transferred out of HMP Garton, how many prisoners will remain?

Answer

Question 26

There are 30 cells on Yellow wing at HMP Garton. Each cell has two beds. How many beds are there on Yellow wing?

Answer

Question 27

There are 34 tables in the dining area of HMP Garton.
Of these:

- 4 tables have 3 chairs each;

- 10 tables have 6 chairs each;

- 8 tables have 7 chairs each;

- 12 tables have 9 chairs each.

How many chairs are there in total?

Answer

Question 28

36 prison officers work at HMP Orion. Of these, 75% are
male. How many male prison officers are there at HMP
Orion?

Answer

Question 29

A prisoner at HMP Orion earns 68p per day for working in
the laundry room. How much does he earn if he works for 6
days?

Answer

Question 30

A prisoner at HMP Orion earns 71p per day for working in the workshop. How much does he earn if he works for 17 days?

Answer

Question 31

A prisoner at HMP Orion earns £1.05 per day for working in the kitchen. How much does he earn if he works for 9 days?

Answer

Question 32

A prisoner at HMP Orion works in the workshop for 2.5 hours every morning and 4.5 hours every afternoon for 5 days a week. How many hours does he work in total over a 3-week period?

Answer

Question 33

A prisoner at HMP Orion works in the library for 4.5 hours every morning and 3.5 hours every afternoon for 3 days a week. How many hours does he work in total over an 8-week period?

Answer

Item	Cost of the item	Number sold
Shoe polish	£1.37	7
Talcum powder	£0.98	9
Mars bars	£0.56	19
Can of coke	£0.74	23

Your line manager has asked you to complete an order for some new stock in the prison officers' shop.

Question 34

According to the table, how much has been spent on shoe polish?

Answer

Question 35

According to the table, how much has been spent on talcum powder?

Answer

Question 36

According to the table, how much has been spent on Mars bars?

Answer

Question 37

According to the table, how much has been spent on cans of coke?

Answer

Question 38

According to the table, how much has been spent on all four items in total?

Answer

Question 39

It takes a prison officer 10 minutes to search one cell. How many cells can he search in 5 hours?

Answer

Question 40

A prison officer can search a total of 15 visitors in one hour. How long would it take him to search 90 visitors?

Answer

ANSWERS TO SAMPLE PRISON OFFICER SELECTION TEST (POST) NUMBER 2

1.	£3.00	**21.**	375
2.	9	**22.**	15
3.	1907 hrs, 1835 hrs	**23.**	29
4.	Lines 2,4 and 8	**24.**	252
5.	Macintosh, Davies	**25.**	232
6.	Armstrong, Savage	**26.**	60
7.	Nobody	**27.**	236
8.	Lines 1,2,3,8,10	**28.**	27
9.	78	**29.**	£4.08
10.	34	**30.**	£12.07
11.	32	**31.**	£9.45
12.	32	**32.**	105 hrs
13.	6:1	**33.**	192 hrs
14.	72	**34.**	£9.59
15.	52	**35.**	£8.82
16.	184	**36.**	£10.64
17.	203	**37.**	£17.02
18.	80	**38.**	£46.07
19.	365	**39.**	30 cells
20.	395	**40.**	6 hrs

CHAPTER 7
SAMPLE PRISON OFFICER SELECTION TEST (POST) NUMBER 3

During sample POST number 3 there are 40 questions. You have 20 minutes to complete the test. You are permitted to use a calculator.

Question 1

Prison officers are required to use the 24-hour clock. Convert 2:17am into 24-hour clock?

Answer

Question 2

Prison officers are required to use the 24-hour clock.

Convert 3:08pm into 24-hour clock?

Answer

Question 3

Prison officers are required to use the 24-hour clock. Convert 9:21pm into 24-hour clock?

Answer

Question 4

Prison officers are required to use the 24-hour clock. Convert 11:34pm into 24-hour clock?

Answer

Question 5

Prison officers are required to use the 24-hour clock. Convert 8:59pm into 24-hour clock?

Answer

Question 6

Prison officers are required to use the 24-hour clock. Convert 6:20am into 24-hour clock?

Answer

Question 7

Prison officers are required to use the 24-hour clock.
Convert 12:01am into 24-hour clock?

Answer

Question 8

A prison officer has a 15-minute tea break. If he stops work for his tea break at 3:21pm, what time will he return to work? (Use 24-hour clock)

Answer

Question 9

A prison officer has a 25-minute tea break. If he stops work for his tea break at 7:24pm, what time will he return to work? (Use 24-hour clock)

Answer

Question 10

A prison officer has a 35-minute tea break. If he stops work for his tea break at 11:45pm, what time will he return to work? (Use 24-hour clock)

Answer

Question 11

HMP Rowenstown operates the following system:

09:00 hrs – cells unlocked

11:15 hrs – cells locked

12:50 hrs – cells unlocked

15:10 hrs – cells locked

17:00 hrs – cells unlocked

20:20 hrs – cells locked

How many hours each day are the cells unlocked for?

Answer

Question 2

HMP Dudley operates the following system:

08:30 hrs – cells unlocked

10:20 hrs – cells locked

11:55 hrs – cells unlocked

12:50 hrs – cells locked

15:40 hrs – cells unlocked

18:20 hrs – cells locked

20:20 hrs – cells unlocked

21:40 hrs – cells locked

How many hours each day are the cells locked for?

Answer

Question B

The gymnasium at HMP Riley is open during the following times:

11:20 hrs until 12:45 hrs

18:30 hrs until 21:40 hrs

How many hours each day is the gym open for?

Answer

The following graph shows the number of prisoners at HMP Renton between January and April.

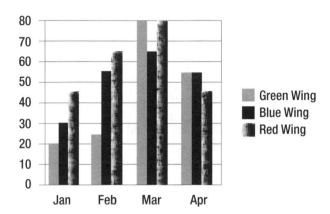

Question 14

How many prisoners were at HMP Renton in total during the four-month period?

Answer

Question 15

In January there were 20 prisoners on Green wing at HMP Renton. During March there were 80 prisoners on Green wing. What percentage increase is this?

Answer [   ]

The following graph shows the number of drug tests and the results at HMP Dodinghurst during 2009.

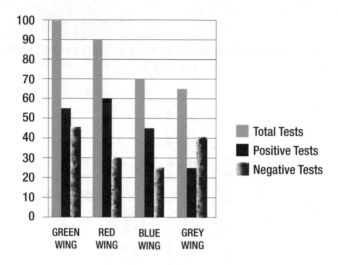

Question 16

How many drug tests were carried out in total during 2009?

Answer [   ]

Question 17

How many positive tests were there in total during 2009?

Answer [   ]

Question 18

How many negative tests were there in total during 2009?

Answer

Question 19

There are 120 staff at HMP Dodinghurst. Of these, 40% are female and 60% are male. How many female members of staff are there at HMP Dodinghurst?

Answer

Question 20

There are 500 prisoners at HMP Smithtown. Of these:

- 200 are remand prisoners
- 75 are life-sentenced prisoners
- 150 are sex offenders
- The remainder are in other categories

What percentage are life-sentenced?

Answer

Question 21

There are 500 prisoners at HMP Smithtown. Of these:

- 200 are remand prisoners
- 75 are life-sentenced prisoners
- 150 are sex offenders
- The remainder are in other categories

What percentage sex offenders?

Answer

Question 22

There are 500 prisoners at HMP Smithtown. Of these:

- 200 are remand prisoners
- 75 are life-sentenced prisoners
- 150 are sex offenders
- The remainder are in other categories

What percentage are in other categories?

Answer [   ]

You have been assigned to Yellow wing at your first prison. List A is the official location of your prisoners. Prisoners can move freely around Yellow wing providing they adhere to the following rules:

RULES:

1. Prisoners in cells A1, A3 and D4 are not allowed in cells A2, D1 or D2.

2. No more than 3 prisoners are allowed in one cell at any one time.

Your supervisory manager has asked you to check the locations of all your prisoners to ensure none of them is breaking the rules.

List A: Official cell locations

A1 Parker, Rose, Stevens	D1 Brown, Janes, Peters
A2 Silvey, Craig	D2 Williams, Hutchinson, Joynes

A3 Hendry, Millington	**D3** Fredricks
A4 Ashley, Pennington	**D4** Smith
A5 Barker, Stevenson, Milliband	**D5** Jones, Ashdown, Minton

List B is the observations you find after your investigation.

List B: Your observations

A1 Parker, Rose, Stevens	**D1** Brown, Janes, Peters, Milliband
A2 Silvey, Smith , Craig	**D2** Williams
A3 Hendry	**D3** Fredricks
A4 Ashley, Pennington	**D4** Hutchinson, Joynes
A5 Barker, Stevenson	**D5** Jones, Ashdown, Minton

Question 23

Is anybody missing? If so, who?

Answer

Question 24

Who is contravening Rule 1?

Answer

Question 25

Who is contravening Rule 2?

Answer

Read the following passage before answering the questions.

A prison officer has responsibility for the security, super-vision, training and rehabilitation of people committed to prison by the courts. This includes motivating prisoners to do what is best for themselves, and others around them, within a safe and healthy environment. In addition to their custodial duties, prison officers must be able to establish and maintain positive working relationships with prisoners, balancing authority with a large amount of understanding and compassion, in order to effect rehabilitation.

The nature of the role demands the ability to think on one's feet, make quick decisions and deal effectively with un-expected situations. Some of the work will vary according to the type of prison and level of security (e.g. category A prisoners require closer supervision than category C). However, typical work activities include:

• performing security checks and search procedures;

• supervising prisoners, keeping an account of those in your charge and maintaining proper order;

• supervising visits and carrying out patrol duties;

• escorting prisoners;

• assisting in prisoner reviews;

• advising and counselling prisoners, making sure they have access to professional help if needed;

• employing authorised physical control and restraint procedures where appropriate;

• taking care of prisoners' property;

• being aware of prisoners' rights, dignity and their personal responsibility;

- providing appropriate care and support for prisoners at risk of self-harm;
- promoting anti-bullying and suicide prevention policies;
- taking an active part in rehabilitation programmes, including workshops;
- assessing and advising prisoners;
- liaising with other specialist staff, including health and social work professionals;
- writing prisoner reports.
- Higher-grade prison officers have extra responsibilities, such as supervising other officers or looking after an area or wing of the prison.

Question 26

The nature of the role demands the ability to think on one's feet, make quick decisions and do what?

Answer

Question 27

Part of the Prison Officers role includes advising and counselling prisoners and making sure they have access to what?

Answer

Question 28

Apart from supervising other officers, higher-grade prison officers might also have the responsibility of looking after what?

Answer

Question 29

Category C prisoners require closer supervision than category A prisoners – True or False?

Answer

Question 30

What type of policies are prison officers required to promote?

Answer

Question 31

A prison officer has responsibility for the security, supervision, training and rehabilitation of people committed to prison by the courts. This includes motivating prisoners to do what is best for themselves, and others around them, within what type of environment?

Answer

Question 32

Compare the following two lists below. Write down the number of the line(s) where you identify a difference between the two lists.

1.	Smith	45	Remand	Dairy free
2.	Jessop	24	Remand	Gluten free
3.	Moore	48	Other	Nut allergy
4.	Matchem	23	Life	Dairy free
5.	Allan	35	Sex offender	Vegan
6.	Halsam	21	Other	Vegetarian
7.	Bolton	29	Life	Dairy free
8.	Carlston	41	Remand	Vegan

1.	Smith	45	Remand	Dairy free
2.	Jesson	24	Remand	Gluten free
3.	Moore	49	Other	Nut allergy
4.	Matchem	23	Life	Dairy free
5.	Allan	35	Sex offender	Vegetarian
6.	Halsam	21	Other	Vegan
7.	Bolton	29	Life	Dairy free
8.	Carlston	40	Remand	Vegan

The following diagram represents prisoners serving at HMP Derry and their different locations.

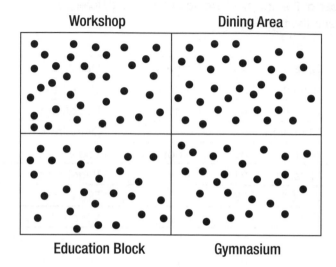

Workshop   **Dining Area**

Education Block   **Gymnasium**

Key: ● = 1 prisoner

Question 33

How many prisoners are there in total?

Answer [   ]

Question 34

How many prisoners are there in Education block and the Dining area?

Answer [   ]

Question 35

If 50% of prisoners in the Workshop go to the Gymnasium, how many prisoners will there now be in the Gymnasium?

Answer

Question 36

If 25% of prisoners leave the Dining area, how many prisoners will there now be in the Dining area?

Answer

The following diagram represents prisoners serving at HMP Frinton and their different locations.

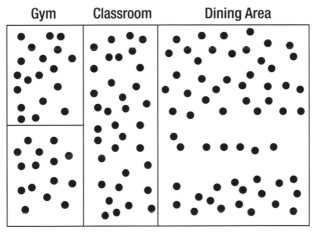

Gym   Classroom   Dining Area

Workshop

Key: ● = 1 prisoner

Question 37

How many prisoners are there in total?

Answer

Question 38

If 70% of prisoners leave the Dining area, how many prisoners will remain in the Dining area?

Answer

Question 39

If a third of prisoners at HMP Frinton are remand prisoners, how many prisoners are not remand prisoners?

Answer

Question 40

If 10% of prisoners in the Dining area move to the classroom, how many prisoners will there now be in the Classroom?

Answer

ANSWERS TO SAMPLE PRISON OFFICER SELECTION TEST (POST) NUMBER 3

1. 02:17 hrs
2. 15:08 hrs
3. 21:21 hrs
4. 23:34 hrs
5. 20:59 hrs
6. 06:20 hrs
7. 00:01 hrs
8. 15:36 hrs
9. 19:49 hrs
10. 00:20 hrs
11. 7 hrs 55 mins
12. 17 hrs 15 mins
13. 4 hrs 35 mins
14. 620
15. 400%
16. 325
17. 185
18. 140
19. 48
20. 15%
21. 30%
22. 15%

23. Millington
24. Smith
25. Milliband
26. Deal effectively with unexpected situations.
27. Professional help if needed.
28. An area or wing of the prison.
29. False
30. Promote anti-bullying and suicide prevention policies.
31. A safe and healthy environment.
32. Lines 2, 3, 5, 6 and 8
33. 117
34. 58
35. 42
36. 24
37. 129
38. 18
39. 86
40. 41

CHAPTER 8
SAMPLE PRISON OFFICER SELECTION TEST (POST) NUMBER 4

During sample POST number 4 there are 40 questions. You have 20 minutes to complete the test. You are permitted to use a calculator.

Question 1

There are 600 prisoners at HMP Watersford and a total of 30 prison officers on duty. What is the ratio of prisoners to prison officers?

Answer

Question 2

At HMP Watersford 30% of prison officers apply for

 how2become

promotion. How many apply?

Answer

Question 3

A prison officer is required to search 40% of all visitors to HMP Watersford. If there are 80 visitors, how many does he have to search?

Answer

Question 4

A prison officer can search six visitors in one hour. How many can he search in 5.5 hours?

Answer

Question 5

Compare the following two lists below. Write down the number of the line(s) where you identify a difference between the two lists.

1	Morrison	44	Remand	Vegetarian
2	Jones	21	Other	Vegetarian
3	Wilcox	26	Life	Dairy free
4	Wallace	29	Remand	Vegan
5	Hardy	30	Sex offender	Dairy free
6	Willshaw	33	Other	Vegan
7	Billings	29	Remand	Dairy free
8	Brimstead	41	Other	Vegetarian

1	Morrsion	44	Remand	Vegetarian
2	Jones	22	Other	Vegetarian
3	Wilcox	26	Life	Dairy free
4	Wallace	29	Sex offender	Vegan
5	Hardy	30	Sex offender	Dairy free
6	Willshaw	33	Remand	Vegan
7	Billings	29	Remand	Dairy free
8	Brimstead	41	Other	Vegan

Answer [   ]

The following diagram represents prisoners serving at HMP Forth and their different locations.

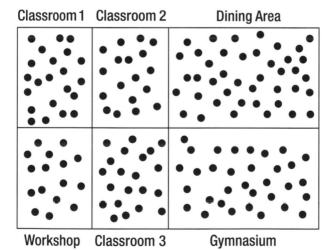

Key: ● = 1 prisoner

Question 6

How many prisoners are there in Classrooms?

Answer

Question 7

How many prisoners are there in the Gymnasium and the Workshop?

Answer

Question 8

If 50% of prisoners in Classroom 1 and 50% of prisoners in Classroom 2 move to the Gymnasium, how many prisoners will there now be in Classrooms?

Answer

Question 9

If there are 19 prison officers on duty at HMP Forth, what is the ratio of prisoners to prison officers?

Answer

You have been assigned to Grey wing at your first prison. List A is the official location of your prisoners. Prisoners can move freely around Grey wing providing they adhere to the following rules:

RULES:

1. Prisoners in cells A3, A5 and D1 are not allowed in cells A1, D3 or D5.

2. No more than 3 prisoners are allowed in one cell at any one time.

3. Prisoners are only allowed to be on their own in their own cell.

Your supervisory manager has asked you to check the locations of all your prisoners to ensure none of them is breaking the rules.

List A: Official cell locations

A1 Miles, Johnson, Carter	D1 Smithson, Hutchinson, Davies
A2 Hudson, Button, Smith	D2 Davis, Rogers
A3 Clipstone, Moore, Price	D3 Stinson, Cartwright, Benson
A4 Jules, Kipp, Manson	D4 Winters, Yore, Trott
A5 French, Barker	D5 Bromley, Wall

List B is the observations you find after your investigation.

List B: Your observations

A1 Miles, Johnson, Carter, Clipstone	D1 Smithson, Hutchinson
A2 Hudson, Button, Smith	D2 Davis, Rogers, French
A3 Barker	D3 Cartwright, Benson, Davies
A4 Jules, Kipp, Manson	D4 Winters, Yore, Trott
A5 Moore, Price	D5 Bromley, Wall

Question 10

Who, if anyone, is missing?

Answer

Question 11

Who, if anyone, is contravening Rule 1?

Answer

Question 12

Who, if anyone, is contravening Rule 2?

Answer

Question 13

Who, if anyone, is contravening Rule 3?

Answer

Question 14

Compare the following two lists below. Write down the number of the line(s) where you identify a difference between the two lists.

10	7816542	21	Powell	Other
9	220847	20	Baker	Vegan
8	891524	34	Hall	Vegan

7	17346189	36	Nutsfield	Vegetarian
6	0002415	31	Mares	Dairy free
5	6175902	39	Harrow	Vegetarian
4	82789023	28	Jules	Dairy free
3	80745821	44	Hunter	Vegetarian

10	7816542	21	Powell	Other
9	220847	20	Baker	Vegan
8	891724	34	Hall	Vegan
7	17346189	36	Nutsfield	Vegan
6	002415	31	Mares	Dairy free
5	6175902	39	Harrow	Vegetarian
4	82789023	38	Jules	Dairy free
3	80745821	44	Hunter	Vegetarian

Answer [   ]

You have been assigned to Blue wing at your first prison. List A is the official location of your prisoners. Prisoners can move freely around Blue wing providing they adhere to the following rules:

RULES:

1. Prisoners in cells A1, A2 and D1 are not allowed in cells A3, D2 or D5.

2. No more than 3 prisoners are allowed in one cell at any one time.

3. Prisoners are only allowed to be on their own in their own cell.

Your supervisory manager has asked you to check the locations of all your prisoners to ensure none of them is breaking the rules.

List A: Official cell locations

A1 Powell, Stuart, Wood	D1 Rimmer, Morris
A2 Greystone, Parker	D2 Johnson, Craig, Sutherland
A3 Slidders, Fretten, Johns	D3 Sumners, Lipton, Potter
A4 Hatton	D4 Comer, Cramer, Hart
A5 Grey, Walters, Porter	D5 Willers, Jenson, Field

List B is the observations you find after your investigation.

List B: Your observations

A1 Powell, Stuart, Jenson	D1 Rimmer, Porter
A2 Greystone, Parker	D2 Johnson, Craig, Sutherland
A3 Slidders, Fretten, Johns, Wood	D3 Sumners, Potter
A4 Comer	D4 Cramer, Hart, Hatton
A5 Grey, Walters	D5 Willers , Field, Morris

Question 15

Who, if anyone, is missing?

Answer [   ]

Question 16

Who, if anyone, is contravening Rule 1?

Answer

Question 17

Who, if anyone, is contravening Rule 2?

Answer

Question 18

Who, if anyone, is contravening Rule 3?

Answer

Question 19

A prison officer can search 9 visitors in one hour. How many can he search in 4 hours?

Answer

Question 20

In total there are 176 prisoners living on a wing of a prison and there are 16 prison officers on duty. What is the ratio of prisoners to prison officers?

Answer

Question 21

In total there are 152 prisoners living on a wing of a prison and there are 8 prison officers on duty. What is the ratio of prisoners to prison officers?

Answer

Question 22

It takes a prison officer 7 minutes to complete one prisoner report sheet. How many can she complete in 2 hours?

Answer

Question 23

At HMP Ingleton there are 80 prison officers. If 20% of prison officers apply for promotion, how many apply?

Answer

Question 24

There are 500 prisoners at HMP Clipton. Of these:

• 200 are below the age of 20;

• 180 are between the ages of 20 and 25;

• 120 are over the age of 25.

What percentage or prisoners at HMP Clipton are below the age of 20?

Answer

Question 25

There are 500 prisoners at HMP Clipton. Of these:

- 200 are below the age of 20;
- 180 are between the ages of 20 and 25;
- 120 are over the age of 25.

What percentage or prisoners at HMP Clipton are between the ages of 20 and 25?

Answer [   ]

Question 26

There are 500 prisoners at HMP Clipton. Of these:

- 200 are below the age of 20;
- 180 are between the ages of 20 and 25;
- 120 are over the age of 25.

What percentage or prisoners at HMP Clipton are over the age of 25?

Answer [   ]

Question 27

There are 300 prisoners at HMP Gorton. Of these:

- 30% are below the age of 20;
- 40% are between the ages of 20 and 25;
- 30% are over the age of 25.

How many prisoners at HMP Gorton are below the age of 20?

Answer

Question 28

There are 300 prisoners at HMP Gorton. Of these:

- 30% are below the age of 20;
- 40% are between the ages of 20 and 25;
- 30% are over the age of 25.

How many prisoners at HMP Gorton are between the ages of 20 and 25?

Answer

Question 29

At your first prison you have been asked to check a random 20% of prisoner mail. There are 140 letters in total. How many letters must you check?

Answer

Question 30

A prison officer is required to supervise prisoners in the gymnasium for 90 minutes. If he starts supervising at 18:10 hours, what time will he finish? (Use 24-hour clock)

Answer

Question 31

A prison officer is required to check a prisoner every 20

minutes. How many times must he check him in a 7-hour period?

Answer

Question 32

A prison officer is required to supervise prisoners in the gymnasium for 110 minutes. If he starts supervising at 17:10 hours, what time will he finish? (Use 24-hour clock)

Answer

Question 33

80 visitors arrive at HMP Frinton. You are required to search 30% of visitors. Each search takes 4 minutes to complete. How long will it take you to search 30% of visitors?

Answer

Question 34

110 visitors arrive at HMP Gorton. You are required to search 40% of the visitors. Each search takes 3 minutes to complete. If you start searching at 14:10 hours, what time will you finish? (Use 24-hour clock)

Answer

Question 35

150 visitors arrive at HMP Daleside. You are required to search 30% of the visitors. Each search takes 4 minutes to

complete. If you start searching at 11:20 hours, what time will you finish? (Use 24-hour clock)

Answer

You have been assigned to Green wing at your first prison. List A is the official location of your prisoners. Prisoners can move freely around Green wing providing they adhere to the following rules:

RULES:

1. Prisoners in cells A1, A2 and A3 are not allowed in cells D1, D2 or D3.

2. No more than 3 prisoners are allowed in cells A1, A4 or D1 at any one time.

3. Prisoners are only allowed to be on their own in their own cell.

Your supervisory manager has asked you to check the locations of all your prisoners to ensure none of them is breaking the rules.

List A: Official cell locations

A1 Monk, Jarvis	**D1** Grimthorpe
A2 Wentworth, Jackson, Smith	**D2** Willis, Wallis
A3 Ahmed, Langley	**D3** Hatwell, Brown, Fredricks
A4 Deverill, Scott	**D4** Fenton, Cedar
A5 Attwell, Grimes	**D5** Leadbetter, Byron

List B is the observations you find after your investigation.

List B: Your observations

A1 Monk	**D1** Grimthorpe, Jarvis
A2 Jackson, Smith	**D2** Willis, Wallis, Wentworth
A3 Ahmed, Langley	**D3** Cedar, Brown
A4 Scott, Byron	**D4** Hatwell
A5 Fredricks	**D5** Leadbetter, Grimes, Attwell

Question 36

Who, if anyone, is missing?

Answer

Question 37

Who, if anyone, is contravening Rule 1?

Answer

Question 38

Who, if anyone, is contravening Rule 2?

Answer

Question 39

Who, if anyone, is contravening Rule 3?

Answer

Question 40

360 people apply to become a prison officer. Of this number, 65% are male and 35% are female. How many female applicants are there?

Answer [   ]

ANSWERS TO SAMPLE PRISON OFFICER SELECTION TEST (POST) NUMBER 4

1. 20:1

2. 9

3. 32

4. 33

5. Lines 1, 2, 4, 6 and 8

6. 61

7. 49

8. 41

9. 8:1

10. Stinson

11. Clipstone and Davies

12. Clipstone

13. Barker

14. Lines 8, 7, 6 and 4

15. Lipton

16. Wood and Morris

17. Wood

18. Comer

19. 36

20. 11:1

21. 19:1

22. 17

23. 16

24. 40%

25. 36%

26. 24%

27. 90

28. 120

29. 28 letters

30. 19:40 hours

31. 21

32. 19:00

33. 96

34. 16:22 hours

35. 14:20 hours

36. Deverill and Fenton

37. Jarvis and Wentworth

38. Nobody

39. Fredricks and Hatwell

40. 126

FINAL TIPS FOR PASSING THE PRISON OFFICER SELECTION TEST

- In the build up to the POST, concentrate on improving your numerical reasoning ability.

- Aim for accuracy and speed. Whilst you do not lose marks for incorrect answers it is important to strive for perfection during your preparation.

- Try practising both with and without a calculator.

- Consider purchasing further numerical reasoning books to aid your preparation.

- Consider trying a number of online POST questions through the website www.how2become.co.uk.

CHAPTER 9
READING COMPREHENSION

During the Recruitment Assessment Day you will be required to carry out a reading comprehension exercise. Basically, you'll need to read text that has been taken from a standard Prison Service source. This could be either from the internet (Prison Service website), Prison Service Orders or manuals.

Whilst you do not need to carry out any pre-assessment preparation for this exercise, you can improve your ability in this test by:

1. Visiting and reading the Prison Service website at:
www.hmprisonservice.gov.uk
Read the information on the website and learn as much as possible about the role of a Prison Officer and also the Prison Service.

2. Take the time to read some of the more important Prison Service Orders relevant to the role of a Prison Officer. These are available at:

www.prisonserviceorders.co.uk
On the following page I have provided you with a sample reading comprehension exercise.

Study the passage for 5 minutes only before answering the questions on the next page. You are not permitted to take notes and you are not permitted to refer back to the passage once the 5 minutes are complete.

SAMPLE READING COMPREHENSION EXERCISE 1

Statement of Purpose
Her Majesty's Prison Service serves the public by keeping in custody those committed by the courts. Our duty is to look after them with humanity and help them lead law-abiding and useful lives in custody and after release.

Our Vision
- To provide the very best prison services so that we are the provider of choice.

- To work towards this vision by securing the following key objectives.

Objectives
To protect the public and provide what commissioners want to purchase by:

- Holding prisoners securely

- Reducing the risk of prisoners re-offending

- Providing safe and well-ordered establishments in which we treat prisoners humanely, decently and lawfully.

In securing these objectives we adhere to the following principles:

Our Principles

In carrying out our work we:

- Work in close partnership with our commissioners and others in the Criminal Justice System to achieve common objectives

- Obtain best value from the resources available using research to ensure effective correctional practice

- Promote diversity, equality of opportunity and combat unlawful discrimination, and

- Ensure our staff have the right leadership, organisation, support and preparation to carry out their work effectively.

© Crown copyright 2004

SAMPLE READING COMPREHENSION EXERCISE 1

Question 1

According to the Statement of Purpose, how does Her Majesty's Prison Service serve the public?

Answer

Question 2

The Prison Service objective is to protect the public by holding prisoners securely, providing safe and well-ordered establishments in which they treat prisoners humanely, decently and lawfully, and what else?

Answer

Question 3

One of the principles of the Prison Service is to promote diversity, equality of opportunity and combat what?

Answer

Question 4

One of the duties of the Prison Service is to help prisoner's lead law-abiding and useful lives in custody and after release. What is the other duty?

Answer

ANSWERS TO SAMPLE READING COMPREHENSION EXERCISE 1

Question 1
By keeping in custody those committed by the courts.

Question 2
Reducing the risk of prisoners re-offending.

Question 3
Unlawful discrimination.

Question 4
Look after them with humanity.

Now that you have completed reading comprehension exercise 1, move on to exercise 2.

SAMPLE READING COMPREHENSION EXERCISE 2

Study the passage for 5 minutes only before answering the questions on the next page. You are not permitted to take notes and you are not permitted to refer back to the passage once the 5 minutes are complete.

Security

The Prison Service is committed to protecting the public. This means holding prisoners securely and pursuing policies to reduce re-offending.

Our core business is keeping prisoners in custody. Security is the bedrock on which all of our

efforts to develop positive regimes are based. We continually strive to improve our excellent

security record, which has seen no escapes by Category A prisoners since 1995.

The prevention of escapes has resulted in more resources being invested in programmes to treat, educate and rehabilitate prisoners.

Security is an all-embracing term. By it we mean:

- Physical security – walls, bars, locks or even more modern devices such as Closed Circuit Television;

- Security procedures – for instance accounting for prisoners or searching cells;

- Assessment procedures – categorising prisoners to make sure that they are kept in appropriate security conditions;

- Intelligence gathering.

Security is also achieved in other ways:

- By diverting prisoners' energy into constructive work and activity

- By developing positive relationships with prisoners

- By creating decent regimes and programmes for prisoners.

© Crown copyright 2004

SAMPLE READING COMPREHENSION EXERCISE 2

Question 1

The Prison Service is committed to protecting the public. This means holding prisoners securely and pursuing policies to reduce what?

Answer

Question 2

The Prison Service continually strives to improve its excellent security record, which has seen no escapes by Category A prisoners since when?

Answer

Question 3

Security is achieved in other ways by diverting prisoners' energy into constructive work and activity, by creating decent regimes and programmes for prisoners, and also by developing what?

Answer

Question 4

Categorising prisoners to make sure that they are kept in appropriate security conditions forms part of which procedures?

Answer [   ]

ANSWERS TO SAMPLE READING COMPREHENSION EXERCISE 2

Question 1
Re-offending.

Question 2
1995.

Question 3
Developing positive relationships with prisoners.

Question 4
Assessment.

TIPS FOR PREPARING FOR THE COMPREHENSION EXERCISE

- In the build up to the Recruitment Assessment Day, take the time to read Prison Service Orders. Whilst not essential, they will give you an insight into the role of a prison officer and also how the Prison Service operates. Many of the extracts used during the reading comprehension exercise are taken from these orders. Visit www.prisonserviceorders.co.uk where you will find a full list.

- Read a newspaper article of interest for five minutes before getting a friend or relative to ask you questions on the content.

CHAPTER 10
RECALLING SEEN INFORMATION

During this test, which forms part of the Recruitment Assessment Day, you will be shown a colour photograph of a prison scene for three minutes. The photograph is then removed and you will be asked a number of questions about what you saw. Note taking is not permitted on this exercise.

I have found that one of the most effective ways to prepare for this test is to carry out exercises that improve your memory. There are a number of products on the market that will serve this purpose such as Brain Trainer.

The key to storing visual information into your memory is concentration; unless you focus on information intently, it will go away and you won't be able to recall it. This is why teachers are always nagging students to pay attention! You need to focus your mind intently on the scene presented in front of you for three minutes solid, taking in all that you see. Let's assume that you are presented with an image of two

prisoners in a prison cell. Things you would focus on might include:

- What are the prisoners doing? Are they sitting down, standing or interacting in a certain way?

- What clothes are the prisoners wearing and what colour are their clothes/shoes?

- Are there any objects in the cell such as a television, sink, cups etc?

- What's on the walls of the prison cell?

- Are there any numbers in the image that you may be asked to recall?

On the following pages I have provided you with a number of exercises that will go a long way to helping you improve your memory.

SAMPLE MEMORY TEST 1

Study the following words for three minutes only. Once the three minutes are complete, turn the page and answer the questions without referring back to words.

Cat	Car	Piano	Motorbike
Love	House	Bark	Snake
Lorry	Pond	Kitten	Bicycle
Drums	Life	Guitar	River
Dog	Lake	Parrot	Flute

SAMPLE MEMORY TEST 1 QUESTIONS

Question I
How many words are there in total?

Answer

Question 2
How many animals are there?

Answer

Question 3
How many objects have wheels?

Answer

Question 4
How many musical instruments are there?

Answer

ANSWERS TO SAMPLE MEMORY TEST 1

Question 1
20

Question 2
5

Question 3
4

Question 4
4

Once you have checked through your answers, move on to sample memory test 2.

SAMPLE MEMORY TEST 2

Study the following shapes for three minutes only. Once the three minutes are complete, answer the questions without referring back to shapes.

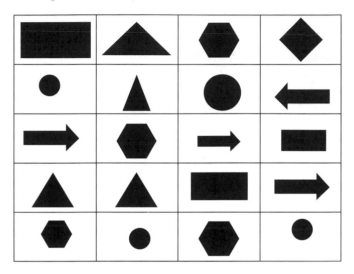

SAMPLE MEMORY TEST 2 QUESTIONS

Question 1

How many shapes are there in total?

Answer

Question 2

How many four sided shapes are there?

Answer

Question 3

How many arrows point to the right?

Answer

Question 4

How many triangles are there?

Answer

ANSWERS TO SAMPLE MEMORY TEST 2

Question 1
20

Question 2
4

Question 3
3

Question 4
4

Once you have checked through your answers, move on to sample memory test 3.

SAMPLE MEMORY TEST 3

Study the following words and shapes for three minutes only. Once the three minutes are complete, answer the questions without referring back to words or shapes.

Blue	Balloon	Bed	Beer
⬢	◼	▬	▼
Apple	Heart	Run	Green
▬	←	⬣	←
Chisel	Hammer	Red	Pear

SAMPLE MEMORY TEST 3 QUESTIONS

Question I

How many four sided shapes are there in total?

Answer

Question 2

How many words begin with the letter B?

Answer

Question 3

How many arrows point to the right?

Answer

Question 4

How many three-letter words are there?

Answer

ANSWERS TO SAMPLE MEMORY TEST 3

Question 1
4

Question 2
4

Question 3
None

Question 4
3

TIPS FOR PREPARING FOR THE RECALLING VISUAL INFORMATION TEST

- The fact that you are being asked to memorise 'visual' information is a benefit. It is far easier to remember visual items, than items that are in written format. In the build up to your assessment read newspaper articles for three minutes and then get a friend to ask you questions based on the content.

- Pick a photograph from a magazine. Study it for three minutes before getting a friend to ask you questions about the image.

- Consider using a brain-training game or resource. These are fun and they can go a long way to improving your memory ability.

CHAPTER 11
THE RECRUITMENT ASSESSMENT DAY AND THE CORE BEHAVIOUR SKILLS

RECRUITMENT ASSESSMENT DAY

As part of their selection process the Prison Service use the Recruitment Assessment Day (RAD) in order to assess a candidate's ability to perform the role of a Prison Officer.

The RAD consists of four 10-minute role-play simulations completed over a period of approximately one-and-a-half hours. At the assessment day you will also be required to complete the second part of your POST, which tests the following elements:

Completing a standard form - You will complete a standard form using written information provided about a prisoner.

Checking information for discrepancies, errors and omissions - You will compare two lists and identify discrepancies and/ or omissions on the second list.

Applying rules - You will be presented with two lists: the first shows cells where prisoners belong (sleep) on a prison wing; the second shows where they are currently located on the wing. You will compare the information on these two lists, and apply three rules in order to determine if everyone is present on the wing and who (if anyone) is breaking the rules.

Reading comprehension - You will read text extracted from a standard Prison Service source (e.g. Prison Service Orders, intranet, manuals etc) and then answer questions about the text.

Once you arrive at the assessment centre you will be registered by a member of the Prison Service RAD team and given a brief outline of what the day involves. During the briefing you will have the opportunity to ask any questions that you may have about the day. You will then receive a briefing pack, which contains information about each of the role-play simulations. You will be allowed to make notes, however, you will not be authorised to take the notes into the simulations with you. In between each simulation you will be given time to re-read any notes you may have made and prepare for your next simulation.

Within the briefing pack you need to determine what it is the selection team are looking for from you during each of the simulations. The exact types of simulation vary greatly between each assessment centre but the core behaviours that you are required to demonstrate are the same throughout.

Providing you pay attention to what is required and learn to incorporate the core behaviours into each simulation, you will greatly increase your chances of success. Some of the more common types of simulation are as follows:

• Dealing with a complaint

- Giving constructive criticism

- Taking criticism

- Dealing with a request for help

- Calming somebody down

- Listening with a purpose

Whilst these are quite vague in terms of their description, you can begin to get a feel for the type of simulation you will be up against during the role-play simulations. The most effective way to prepare is to keep an open mind about the type of simulation you will come across and instead focus your mind on and prepare for the core behaviours. After all, these 6 behaviours are what you will be measured against. If you do not demonstrate them then you will not pass the RAD.

During each of the simulations you will be given a non Prison Service based role that you will assume whilst in the assessment room. The Prison Service want to see that you have the potential to deal with specific situations in an effective manner and you will find that the simulations you are asked to deal with are similar to those that a Prison Officer comes across. The Prison Service expect you to be yourself and deal with the simulations in the same way you would deal with similar situations you meet in everyday life. However, there are a number of things that you can do to improve your chances of success on the day, which I will cover on the following pages.

During the assessment simulations you will be assessed on 6 core behaviours, which are indicated as follows:

CORE BEHAVIOUR 1 - Non-Verbal Listening Skills
(How you show that you are listening)

This is your ability to demonstrate, through your body language, facial expressions and general demeanour that you can effectively listen to what other people are saying. In all of the simulations you will be required to listen effectively to what people are saying and demonstrate that you are doing this through a number of ways, as follows:

How to Listen Effectively

Listening is rarely taught in schools because the teachers or education authorities (along with almost everyone else) assume listening is automatic. But effective listening is a skill. Like any other skill, competency in listening is achieved through learning and practice. The scarcity of good listeners is self-perpetuating; if you didn't have good listeners to learn from and (especially) models to emulate, you probably didn't master this form of effective communication.

The Barriers to Effective Listening

Listening takes time or, more accurately, you have to take time to listen. A life programmed with back-to-back commitments offers little leeway for listening. Similarly, a mind constantly buzzing with plans, dreams, schemes and anxieties is difficult to clear. Good listening requires the temporary suspension of all unrelated thoughts. In order to become an effective listener, you have to learn to manage what goes on in your own mind. Technology, for all its glorious gifts, has erected new barriers to listening. Face-to-face meetings and telephone conversations (priceless listening opportunities) are being replaced by email. Meanwhile television continues to capture countless hours that might otherwise be available for conversation, dialogue and listening.

Ten steps to effective listening during the role-play simulations

1. Face the role-play actor and maintain eye contact.

2. Use facial expressions and simple body language to show the role-play actor that you are listening to them.

3. Keep an open mind when dealing with each scenario.

4. Listen to the words and try to picture what the role-play actor is saying.

5. Don't interrupt and don't impose your solutions.

6. Wait for the role-play actor to pause before asking clarifying questions, unless of course they use inappropriate language or behaviour.

7. Ask questions only to ensure understanding of something that has been said (avoiding questions that disrupt the role-play actor's train of thought).

8. Try to feel what the role-play actor is feeling.

9. Give the role-play actor regular feedback, e.g. summarise, reflect feelings, or simply say "uh huh".

10. Pay attention to what isn't said - to feelings, facial expressions, gestures, posture and other non-verbal cues.

CORE BEHAVIOUR 2 - Suspending Judgement
(How and when to make judgements)

This is all about the timing of your decisions or judgements. How far do you let something go or carry on for before making your judgement? You will need to listen to the information that you are receiving from the simulation and make a decision about when you interact. For example, if you were witnessing a simulation that involved a bullying or harassment situation, then you would want to make your judgement quickly. However, if you were confronted in the simulation with a situation that involved somebody making a

complaint, then you would need to use your effective listening skills for making any judgements. In other words, you need to decide how much information you want to gather before you make a decision or intervene.

CORE BEHAVIOUR 3- Assertion
(Making your argument without being aggressive or yielding)

This is quite a difficult 'skill' to master but one that is important if you are to pass the RAD. Try to think of how you would react if somebody tried to start a fight with you in the pub for no apparent reason. Would you argue with them and make the situation worse? Or would you deal with the situation in a calm but effective manner, with the emphasis on avoiding making the situation worse by instead using effective defusing skills? With any simulation that requires this core behaviour, you must learn to be assertive and firm without coming across as aggressive. This may mean that you need to raise your voice above the person who is shouting at you, but make sure you don't shout aggressively or in a yielding manner. Stay very calm and make sure your body language shows this. Any sign of aggression on your part will not gain you any points.

CORE BEHAVIOUR 4 - Showing Understanding
(How you demonstrate empathy)

What is empathy? Empathy is basically the feeling of concern and understanding for another's situation or feelings. First of all you will need to listen effectively to what the situation involves during the simulation. For example, if someone is making a complaint that they have been bullied or harassed then you will need to demonstrate empathy.

Try to sense others' feelings and take an active interest in their concerns. This can be achieved by both your non-verbal communication or body and language and also your

verbal communication. Phrases such as "That must be very difficult for you" or "I can appreciate what you must be going through right now" demonstrate a person's empathy towards another's unfortunate situation. However, this can only be achieved by including effective facial expressions or body language. For example, if you were responding with these phrases whilst 'yawning', it wouldn't be very effective and would have the opposite effect!

CORE BEHAVIOUR 5 - Exploring and Clarifying
(How you establish information)

During your simulation assessment you will need to ask questions in order to find out what has happened in a situation. For example, if somebody has made a complaint about a specific situation you will need to ask them questions. Probing questions such as "Where did that happen?", "What time did the incident occur?", "Was anybody else involved?", "Who was involved?" will all give you information that was probably not initially forthcoming.

Whatever the simulation you are confronted with, ask probing questions to gather the information you need in order to make effective judgements and decisions.

CORE BEHAVIOUR 6 - Respect for Diversity
(How you demonstrate respect for all people)

Respect for everybody within society and the workplace is very important. Respect for a person's religious beliefs, sexual orientation, race, colour, age etc, is fundamental to the Prison Officer's role.

How would you react in a simulation if you were confronted by a gay person who wanted to make a complaint about how somebody had treated them? If you do not have respect for diversity then you should not be applying for the role

of a Prison Officer. However, there is much you can do to learn about this particular subject and we recommend you read the Race Relations Act 2000, which can be found on the Commission for Racial Equality website. This will give you an insight into the legal requirements now placed on public sector organisations such as the Police Service, Fire Service and Prison Service etc. During all of the simulations remember to have total respect for diversity.

Role-Play Advice

Following the initial welcome briefing, you will be given a briefing on each of the role-play situations that you will have to deal with, during which you will be able to take notes. Although you will not be allowed to take the notes into the simulations with you, you will be given time to re-read them between simulations to prepare yourself for the next role-play.

When you enter the simulation room you will be alone with one role-player.

Role-players can be Prison Officers, other unified grades or actors who are all fully trained to enact scripted role specifications accurately and consistently. A camera will also be in the room. The camera will be inconspicuous and allows for assessors to observe and video the simulation from another room.

Whilst your performance will be assessed as each role-play takes place, if an assessor is uncertain about your performance, they can review this from the video footage before making a final decision. Taking videos of the role-plays also allows for assessors' ratings to be independently checked and monitored.

This quality control measure ensures that all candidates are treated fairly and consistently. Your assessors will be Prison Officers and other uniformed grades. All assessors have completed extensive training and adhere to strict predetermined marking criteria guidelines.

Each role-play simulation lasts for a maximum of 10 minutes. You will be expected to be yourself and deal with the situations in the same way that you would deal with them in everyday life. You will not require experience of working within a prison environment to successfully complete the RAD, as all role-play simulations are non-prison based, although they are similar to situations that prison officers would be expected to deal with. Once the role-play simulations have been completed you will undertake a final briefing session, where you will be given the opportunity to raise any further questions and advised on when your RAD results will be issued.

"Success during the role-plays is really dependent on showing that you can keep a level head in con-frontational situations, can take in what is happening around you, not making snap judgements about people and also that you are able to respect diversity."

Serving Prison Service recruitment staff

TOP TIPS

- Be yourself, remain calm; remember that if the role-player shouts at you (and they will), it is not directed at you personally, but more a sign of their anger and frustration at a situation.

- Let the role-play actor get it out of their system, but don't allow them to swear and be rude to you, say something

along the lines of 'Please don't use that kind of language', but don't let it develop into an argument. Once you have explained the situation, they will calm down and listen to your point of view.

- They look primarily at how you manage the situation. Did you get as much information from the role-player as you could, did you ask questions to clarify points, did you summarise at the end so that it was clear what was going to be done?

- In many of the exercises, there is no right answer, but they are interested in how you reached the conclusion that you arrived at.

- Listen carefully to what is being said both during the brief and during each simulation.

- Practise your core behaviour skills prior to attending the RAD during everyday events.

- Practise your effective listening skills, both non-verbal and verbal.

- Practise non-verbal listening skills in front of the mirror. You should be able to tell how effective your body language and facial expressions are by just looking in the mirror.

- Think about how you would react in a confrontational situation. You need to make sure you can stay calm under pressure and have the ability to defuse any situation. If you feel a situation getting out of hand, don't panic but rather stay calm.

During the next section of the guide I will provide you with a number of sample role-play scenarios, including advice on how to deal with them.

CHAPTER 12
SAMPLE ROLE-PLAY SCENARIOS AND HOW TO DEAL WITH THEM

During this section of the guide I will provide you with a number of sample role-play scenarios and tips on how to deal with each of them in accordance with the six core behavioural skills.

The scenarios provided are all non-prison based. However, they are similar to the types of scenarios you could face as a prison officer.

Following each scenario I have provided you with a template so that you can make notes on how you might personally deal with the scenario. This will allow you to think constructively about the situation you are presented with. When making notes try to consider each of the six core behavioural skills.

Important note: the following sample scenarios will differ from the ones you will be presented with during the Recruitment Assessment Day.

SAMPLE ROLE PLAY SCENARIO 1

You are the manager at a fictitious retail centre. A member of your staff (the role-play actor) approaches you and tells you that another member of staff has been making racist comments about her. She is feeling very upset about the situation and feels threatened by the alleged abuse. She would like to make a complaint.

How to Prepare for the Scenario

To begin with you need to read the briefing pack. What does it tell you about the scenario and are there any clues that dictate how you should respond to the situation? Remember to look at the six core behavioural skills that you are being assessed against. In this instance you will certainly need to demonstrate 'non-verbal listening' skills. This can be done by utilising effective body language and facial expressions. The person has clearly had a terrible experience and you need to reflect this in your response.

As a prison officer you will be required to deal with situations like this. It is important to treat it seriously, take notes relevant to the facts and deal with it quickly and appropriately. Remember to respect diversity at all times.

Once you have listened to what the role actor is saying, you will need to ask probing questions 'exploring and clarifying' exactly what has happened before you make a judgement.

Now take a look at the following sample response to this role-play scenario.

Dealing with Sample Role Play Scenario 1

"Hello, thank you for coming to see me today. I understand you've had a bad experience? I'd like to explore what has happened. Please can you tell me exactly what has happened to you?"

Listen very carefully to what is being said and show that you are listening, both verbally and non-verbally. Don't forget to use facial expressions to demonstrate that you are listening effectively. Nod your head and confirm that you understand what is being said. Just by saying "That must have been terrible for you", you are demonstrating the core skill of 'showing understanding'.

"That must have been terrible for you, are you okay for me to ask you some questions about the situation? If at any time you feel uncomfortable please stop me and we will take a break."

"What did the person say to you?"

"When and where did this happen?"

"How did that make you feel?"

"Have they said anything like this to you before?"

"Are you aware of anybody else receiving the same treatment?"

Once you have gathered these initial facts you will need to clarify what has happened. I suggest you use the word 'clarify' when interacting with the role actor. This will demonstrate to the assessors that you are meeting the core behavioural skill of 'exploring and clarifying'.

"OK, before I make any decisions I'd like to clarify exactly what has happened. You say that you have been bullied for a few weeks now and that it is the same person?"

Once you have gathered the facts of the incident it is important to state that this kind of behaviour is not tolerated and that it will be dealt with effectively. Remember that one of the core behavioural skills is 'respect for race and diversity'.

No form of bullying or harassment should be tolerated and it should be dealt with quickly and effectively.

"Thank you for the information you have provided me with today. I can assure you that this kind of behaviour will not be tolerated and a full investigation will be carried out. In the meantime, in order to protect you from any further harm, I will take you away from the place of danger and allocate another supervisory manager to keep a regular check on you. Please don't hesitate in coming to see me if anything else happens."

Tips for handling the scenario

- Don't forget to cover every core behavioural skill during the scenario. The scenario will last for 10 minutes so you will need to interact with the role actor. You have plenty of time to 'suspend judgement', so use the time wisely.

- Use facial expressions and words to demonstrate that you understand what the person is going through. This is very important.

- Use open body language and face the role actor.

- Use keywords and phrases when communicating with the role actor that are relevant to the core behavioural skills, e.g. "I want to explore further what has happened here." "Let me clarify exactly what has happened."

Now use the template to make notes on how you would deal with this situation.

TEMPLATE FOR SAMPLE SCENARIO I

SAMPLE ROLE-PLAY SCENARIO 2

A friend (the role actor) approaches you and tells you that he is in great financial difficulty. He asks you to lend him some money in order to help him out. He is feeling depressed and suicidal and doesn't know which way to turn. He says he has thought about 'ending it all' and he really needs your help.

How to Prepare for the Scenario

As a prison officer you will need to deal with situations where prisoners are depressed and suicidal. Remember that you will be assessed on a number of areas including showing understanding, assertion, non-verbal communication skills, and exploring and clarifying.

This type of scenario requires skill in all of the above areas. To lend the friend the money would just make his situation worse, but at the same time not lending him the money could exacerbate his depression. How would you deal with the situation? Think carefully about each of the core behavioural skills. If you decide not to lend the friend the money, what alternative action could you take to help him? Is there a possibility that your friend could become verbally aggressive if you refuse to lend him the money? If so, then you will need to deal with the situation assertively.

Now take a look at the following sample response to this role-play scenario.

Dealing with Sample Role Play Scenario 2

"Hello, how are you feeling? I understand that things aren't too good for you at the moment? Tell me what the problem is."

Remember to listen carefully to what is being said. You may need to ask further questions in order to get the information

from the actor. Use effective listening skills and show a non-confrontational stance/body language. Once you have gathered the facts, now is the time to clarify the situation and demonstrate empathy/understanding.

> *"So you're in financial difficulty at the moment? That must be terrible for you? How long has the problem been going on? Have you tried to get professional help for this? Does anybody else know about your situation? I fully appreciate how difficult it must be for you. We need to look at different ways we can resolve this issue without you having to borrow even more money. I want to help you and support you through this difficult time but I'm not prepared to lend you any money as it will just make the situation worse."*

At this point the role actor may become verbally aggressive, simply due to the fact that you are refusing to lend him the money. It is at this point that you will need to be assertive. If the role actor starts to swear or uses inappropriate language, then it is important that you stop it straight away. Let's assume that the role actor has been verbally aggressive towards you.

> *"That kind of language is not acceptable so please do not use it. I am here to help you, but in different ways to lending you more money. This will just place you further into debt. We can work together to look at alternative ways to resolve the issue, possibly looking at professional help? Are you happy for us to do this? Remember that I'm here for you and will support you through this difficult time. You can contact me at any time for support or advice, or even if you just need somebody to talk to."*

Tips for handling the scenario
• Don't forget to cover every core behavioural skill during

the scenario. The scenario will last for 10 minutes so you will need to interact with the role actor. Once again you will need to suspend judgement.

- Scenarios of this nature could have the potential to develop into an argument. The role actor may become verbally aggressive towards you. If this happens it is crucial that you remain calm, keep an open stance and be assertive in your responses. Remember, being assertive does not mean shouting or being aggressive.

- Listen carefully to what the role actor is telling you. If they repeat a piece of information, then it usually has strong significance to the situation.

- Use facial expressions and words to demonstrate that you understand what the person is going through. This is very important.

- Use open body language and face the role actor. Even if the role actor becomes confrontational, maintain an open stance and be calm at all times.

- Use keywords and phrases when communicating with the role actor that are relevant to the core behavioural skills, e.g. "I want to explore further what has happened here." "Let me clarify exactly what has happened."

Now use the template to make notes on how you would deal with this situation.

TEMPLATE FOR SAMPLE SCENARIO 2

SAMPLE ROLE-PLAY SCENARIO 3

You are working as a shop assistant and you are approached by a customer (the role actor) who is not happy with the level of service she has received. She wants to make a complaint.

How to Prepare for the Scenario

During the role-plays you are more than likely to encounter a simulation that involves an angry, confrontational person. The scenario itself is irrelevant; the way you deal with it is the main priority and this is how you'll be assessed.

You may walk into the role-play room and find that the role actor immediately starts shouting at you, so be prepared for such an event and don't get caught out. Before I explain how you can deal effectively with this type of situation, I will explain what not to do:

Standing in a confrontational manner

The natural reaction for many candidates in this type of situation is to meet 'fire with fire'. As soon as the role actor becomes confrontational, they become confrontational back. Of course, this is exactly what the situation is intended to draw out – those candidates who easily become aggressive. As a prison officer you cannot become aggressive back towards inmates. Yes, you need to be firm and assertive, but you must never become confrontational. This will just exacerbate the situation.

During the role-play scenario, stand facing the role actor with an open stance. Do not cross your arms or puff your chest out! Remember that the scenario is not real. They just want to see that you can remain calm, be assertive and that you don't become verbally or physically aggressive.

Shouting back at the role actor

This is something that many applicants in the past have

done. Once the role actor starts shouting, they start shouting back. Avoid this at all costs. Yes it is important to raise your voice in order to be assertive, but do not lose control of the situation. You are the person who needs to be in control of the situation at all times.

Failing to tackle inappropriate language or swearing

At some point during one of the role-play scenarios the actor will use either inappropriate or discriminatory language. It is crucial that you challenge it immediately. One of the assessable areas is respect for race and diversity. As soon as the role actor makes derogatory comments, swears, or becomes verbally abusive, then you need to challenge it in a calm but firm manner. For example:

"Please do not use that kind of language. I am here to help you but I will not tolerate language of that nature."

Remember; always be in control of the situation. As soon as the role actor swears or uses inappropriate language, an alarm bell should ring in your mind that indicates you need to take action.

Your assertion in such scenarios is an area that will be assessed and you need to stand your ground. As a prison officer you will need to defuse confrontational situations, possibly on a daily basis, and this type of scenario will test your ability to do just that.

Dealing with Sample Role Play Scenario 3

"Hello, I understand there's a problem, please can you tell me what has happened?"

The role actor immediately becomes confrontational, shouting at the top of her voice, swearing and also making derogatory comments about the person from a different background who served her. You respond in an 'assertive'

manner and also in a way that shows 'respect for race and diversity' by saying:

"Please don't use that kind of language. I am here to help you and will do all that I can to assist but please try to calm down. I won't accept swearing or language of that nature in relation to members of staff. Please refrain from using it."

The role actor continues to speak with a raised voice. At this point you decide to let them get the problem of their chest. Whilst they are talking, you maintain an open body stance and demonstrate effective communication skills by nodding your head and acknowledging what they are saying. At this point you are demonstrating the core behaviour skill of 'suspending judgement'. However, if they swear again, or use inappropriate language, then you must challenge it.

Once they have finished speaking you decide to 'explore' the situation a little further:

"OK, thanks for providing me with that information. I just want to explore a few more things in order to establish the facts..."

Once they have answered all of your questions, it is now time to 'clarify' and 'show understanding'.

"Thanks for sharing that information with me. I fully understand how you must be feeling; it can't be easy for you. I will do everything that I can to resolve this issue quickly. Let me clarify what has happened..."

Once you have clarified the facts of the matter, you decide to resolve it.

"This has been a difficult time for you and I understand how you must be feeling. In order to rectify this problem I will..."

Situations of this nature are probably the toughest to deal with. However, if you remember to stay calm and focus on the six core behavioural skills, as demonstrated above, then you will be fine. Take a look at the following tips on how to handle this type of situation.

Tips for handling the situation

- Be prepared for a confrontational situation as soon as you enter the room. There will be at least one of this nature out of the four that you are required to deal with.

- This type of scenario is designed to get an immediate confrontational reaction from you. Remember to stay calm and never become confrontational.

- Don't take any comments that are made by the role actor personally.

- Listen carefully to what is being said.

- Remember to concentrate on the six core behavioural skills.

- Use effective judgement to decide when to intervene. Always tackle swearing and inappropriate language immediately.

- Avoid physical touching. There is no need to touch the role actor.

- Try to defuse the situation in a calm manner.

- Use open body language.

- Be assertive in your responses and slightly raise your voice if appropriate but never shout.

- Use phrases such as 'please calm down', 'being aggressive will not get this problem sorted', and 'let's work together to try to resolve this issue.'

TEMPLATE FOR SAMPLE SCENARIO 3

SAMPLE ROLE-PLAY SCENARIO 4

Whilst working as a prison officer at your first prison, a prisoner (the role actor) has been contravening rules by:

• Bullying new inmates and swearing at other prisoners;

It is your responsibility to talk to him about his behaviour with a view to rectifying these problems. He is a relatively new inmate himself and has been finding it difficult to settle into prison life.

How to Prepare for the Scenario

This type of exercise requires you to gather information and ask probing questions as to why these incidents are occurring. Whilst you will need to be firm with the individual concerned and his behaviour should not be tolerated, you will also need to explore whether there are any underlying problems causing him to act in this manner. Maybe he has personal problems or there may be other issues at the centre of the problem. Remember that one of the assessable core behaviour skills is that of 'exploring and clarifying'.

As a prison officer you will be faced with situations like this on a regular basis. Situations are not always what they appear to be on face value. You will need to use your own judgements and assess the situation accordingly; acting on the information you receive from the role actor.

Dealing with Sample Role Play Scenario 4

"Hi, thanks for coming to see me. I'd like to talk to you about an issue that has been brought to my attention. It's been noticed that you've been bullying some of the new inmates and also swearing at other prisoners. What's been making you act in this manner?"

As soon as the prisoner starts talking to you he breaks down crying and he is clearly upset at something. It is important

that you 'show understanding' at this stage before 'exploring' what the real problem is.

"Hey, wha*t's the problem? Tell me what's on your mind and how you're fee*ling? I fully understand this is difficult for you but you need to talk and get things off your chest."

The prisoner (role actor) starts to open up to you. He explains that he recently received a letter from his girlfriend at home telling him that their relationship was over. He feels angry about this and has started to take it out on the other prisoners and new inmates. Your task now is to once again 'show understanding' towards his situation and further 'explore' his feelings and the situation. Once you have done this, and you have 'clarified' his situation, you will need to explain that his behaviour is not acceptable despite his bad fortune. This must be done in a sensitive manner.

"Oh no, that's terrible news and I'm really sorry to hear that. I can understand the anger that you must be feeling. However, as you can appreciate, your actions towards the other prisoners aren't acceptable. It's at times like these that you need the support of other people and you can gain that support by treating people with respect. Can you understand that?"

If the prisoner (role actor) doesn't agree with you then you will need to further explain the situation using a level of 'assertion'. Once he agrees then you can further offer support by saying:

"This is clearly a difficult time that you are going through. I'm here for you to talk to whenever you need. Instead of shouting at other prisoners, come and sit down and talk to me about your feelings. Are you happy with that?"

Being a prison officer is about providing appropriate support for prisoners when needed. It is not about shouting at them or punishing them for their crimes. The focus is on following rules and policies, and also on rehabilitation.

Tips for handling the situation

- Your priority is to support the prisoner (role actor) and to prevent these incidents from happening again.

- If the role actor becomes visibly distressed and upset then you will need to offer your support by talking to them and getting them to open up.

- Show a level of understanding and empathy where appropriate.

- If the role actor starts to swear or uses inappropriate language then you will need to challenge it assertively.

- Make sure you tackle the problem of bullying and swearing. Whilst you will need to offer support to the role actor, the main priority is to stop the bullying.

TEMPLATE FOR SAMPLE SCENARIO 4

SAMPLE ROLE-PLAY SCENARIO 5

Whilst working as a line manager in an office, a member of staff has been laughing and making fun of one of the other members of staff who has a disability. He has been calling him names and tampering with his wheelchair. The victim has made a complaint and it is your responsibility to speak to the offender and take appropriate action.

How to Prepare for the Scenario

This type of scenario is designed to assess your assertiveness and your ability to stop behaviour that is inappropriate. It is imperative that behaviour of this nature is stopped immediately. It is also important that you explore and clarify in order to ascertain the facts of the incidents and also why the person is behaving as they are.

Don't forget to concentrate on the six core behaviours at all times during the role-play scenario.

Dealing with Sample Role Play Scenario 5

"Hi, thanks for coming to see me today. I've been made aware of recent incidents that involve you making fun of another member of staff who has a disability. Please can you tell me what has happened?"

The role actor will start to explain his version of events and what has happened. The role actor explains that it was all just a bit of fun and that the person in the wheelchair likes it because it makes him the centre of attention. He says that no harm is intended and it's all a good laugh. If you ask him to stop doing it then he believes it will affect team morale. Once you have 'explored' a little further, you decide to say:

"Whilst I appreciate morale in the office is important, it is not at the expense of others' misfortune. Even though

the person might appear to like it, it can have devastating effects on how they feel and perform at work. This kind of behaviour is not tolerated and due to the severity of it I am going to place you on a warning. Do you understand?"

The role actor now starts to disagree with you, swearing and being verbally abusive in the process. It is important at this stage that you stay calm, maintain an open body stance and stand firm by your decision.

*"That kind of language is not tolerated so please do not use it. It is impo*rtant that you understand fully the implications of your actions towards other people and I stand by my decision to place you on a warning. I do not want to see this kind of behaviour again and will be monitoring the situation in the future."

Tips for handling the situation

- Any form of bullying or harassment must be dealt with effectively. Do not let it pass by or ignore it. If the role actor tries to persuade you otherwise, you must stand firm.

- Stay calm during the scenario and always remain in control.

- If the role actor starts to swear or uses inappropriate language then you will need to challenge it assertively.

- In the above example, I have placed the role actor on a warning. Is this essential? You will need to judge each case as it happens but I believe in this case it is important to demonstrate assertiveness and that you have the ability to challenge bullying and harassment effectively. Remember that one of the core behaviour skills is that of respect for race and diversity.

TEMPLATE FOR SAMPLE SCENARIO 5

SAMPLE ROLE-PLAY SCENARIO 6

You are a local Housing Association Officer and you are called to a house where a lady has damaged a neighbour's fence.

Any tenants who deliberately damage council property are liable to criminal proceedings. It is your responsibility to speak to the lady and take whatever action you feel appropriate in the circumstances.

How to Prepare for the Scenario

This type of situation is designed to assess your ability to explore, clarify and suspend judgement. It is important as a prison officer that you have the ability to gather the facts first as opposed to jumping to conclusions. On face value, this type of situation looks like the lady has damaged the fence on purpose, and therefore is liable to criminal proceedings.

Many candidates would be tempted to jump in and take firm, assertive action. Make sure you explore the facts fully before deciding on the appropriate course of action.

Dealing with Sample Role Play Scenario 6

"Hello Madam, I am the local Housing Association Officer and I am here to talk to you about a neighbour's fence that you allegedly damaged. Please can you tell me exactly what has happened?"

It is important to 'explore' the facts first. This opening statement allows you to stand there and listen carefully to what the role actor has to say. The lady starts off by explaining she was having a party when the fence was damaged. She was having a few friends round to cheer her up because she is having a bad time at the moment and they had a few drinks too many.

This is a good time to explore further what the problem is. The clue from the role actor is in her statement where she states her friends came round to 'cheer her up because she is having a bad time at the moment'.

"I'm sorry to hear that you're having a bad time at the moment. You say that your friends came round to cheer you up. Is there anything I can do to help? Is everything alright?"

The lady then explains that her partner recently left her and that she doesn't have much money. However, she is prepared to pay for the damage she has caused to the fence. You may then decide to say:

"Thank you for offering to pay for the fence to be repaired. I will speak to the neighbour and mention this too him. However, because money is tight at the moment, do you not have a friend who could maybe fix the fence for you?"

By saying this you are showing a good level of understanding to the tenant's situation and trying to help her with her financial situation. At the end of the scenario you may wish to say:

"Thank you for agreeing to co-operate. If there's anything I can do to help then please call me at the office."

Tips for handling the situation
- Listen carefully to what is being said and use effective non-verbal communication skills.

- Ask questions to explore and clarify.

- Show a level of understanding where appropriate.

TEMPLATE FOR SAMPLE SCENARIO 6

CHAPTER 13
HOW TO GET PRISON OFFICER FIT

INTRODUCTION

Within this guide I have provided you with a number of useful exercises that will allow you to prepare for, and pass, the Prison Officer fitness tests.

The Prison Officer fitness test is not too difficult to pass, providing you put in the time and effort to reach a good all-round level of fitness. Prison Officers need to have a reasonable level of aerobic fitness and also a good level of strength and stamina. The exercises contained within this guide will help you to achieve exactly that. Do not spend hours in the gym lifting heavy weights as the job does not require that level of strength, but rather aim for a varied and diverse fitness programme that covers exercises such as swimming, rowing, jogging, brisk walking and light weight work.

In addition to getting fit, keep an eye on your diet and try to eat healthy foods whilst drinking plenty of water. It will all go

a long way to helping you improve your general well-being and concentration levels whilst you prepare for the selection process.

PLANNING YOUR WORKOUTS AND PREPARING FOR THE PRISON OFFICER FITNESS TESTS

Most people who embark on a fitness regime in January have given it up by February. The reason why most people give up their fitness regime so soon is mainly due to a lack of proper preparation. You will recall that throughout the duration of this guide the word preparation has been integral, and the same word applies when preparing for the fitness tests. Preparation is key to your success and it is essential that you plan your workouts effectively.

To begin with, try to think about the role of a Prison Officer and what it entails. You will have to run quickly on some occasions and you will also need a level of strength for certain operational tasks. In the build-up to the fitness tests I advise that you concentrate on specific exercises that will allow you to pass the tests with ease. Read on for some great ways to pass the Prison Officer fitness tests and stay fit all year round.

Get an assessment before you start training

The first step is to get a fitness test at the gym, weigh yourself and run your fastest mile. Once you have done all three of these you should write down your results and keep them hidden away somewhere safe. After a month of following your new fitness regime, do all three tests again and check your results against the previous month's. This is a great way to monitor your performance and progress and it will also keep you motivated and focused on your goals.

Keep a check on what you eat and drink

Make sure you write down everything you eat and drink for a whole week. You must include tea, water, milk, biscuits and anything and everything that you digest. You will soon begin to realise how much you are eating and you will notice areas in which you can make some changes. For example, if you are taking sugar with your tea then why not try reducing it or giving it up altogether. If you do then you will soon notice the difference.

It is important that you start to look for opportunities to improve your fitness and well-being right from the offset. These areas are what I call 'easy wins'.

Exercises that will help you to pass the fitness tests

It is my strong belief that you do not have to attend a gym in order to prepare for the Prison Officer fitness tests. If I was applying today then I would embark on a fitness programme that included brisk walking, running, press-ups, sit-ups, squats and lunges. In order to improve my upper body strength I would also go swimming.

Walking is one of the best exercises you can do as part of your preparation for the fitness tests. Whilst it shouldn't be the only form of exercise you carry out, it will go a long way to improving your focus and general well-being. Now when I say 'walking' I don't mean a gentle stroll, I mean 'brisk' walking. Try walking at a fast pace for 30 minutes every day for a 7-day period. Then see how you feel at the end of the 7 days. I guarantee you'll begin to feel a lot healthier and fitter. Brisk walking is also a fantastic way to lose weight if you think you need to. In addition to helping you to lose weight it will also keep your concentration and motivational levels up.

There are some more great exercises contained within this guide and most of them can be carried out without the need to attend a gym.

One step at a time

Only you will know how fit you are. I advise that you first of all write down the areas that you believe or feel you need to improve on. For example, if you feel that you need to work on your upper body strength then pick out exercises from this guide that will work on that area for you. I also advise that you obtain a copy of the multi-stage fitness test and practise it. Make sure you can easily pass the required standard.

The key to making improvements is to do it gradually, and at one step at a time. Try to set yourself small goals. If you think you need to lose two stone in weight then focus on losing a few pounds at a time. For example, during the first month aim to lose 6 pounds only. Once you have achieved this then again aim to lose 6 pounds over the next month, and so on and so forth. The more realistic your goal, the more likely you are to achieve it. One of the biggest problems people encounter when starting a fitness regime is that they become bored quickly. This then leads to a lack of motivation and desire, and soon the fitness programme stops.

Change your exercise routine often. Instead of walking try jogging. Instead of jogging try cycling with the odd day of swimming. Keep your workouts varied and interesting to ensure that you stay focused and motivated.

STRETCHING

How many people stretch before carrying out any form of exercise? Very few people, is the correct answer! Not only is it irresponsible but it is also placing you at high risk from injury. Before I commence with the exercises we will take a look at a few warm-up stretches. Make sure you stretch fully before carrying out any exercises. You want your Prison Officer career to be a long one and that means looking after

yourself, including stretching! It is also very important to check with your GP that you are medically fit to carry out any form of physical exercise.

The warm-up calf stretch
To perform this stretch effectively you should first of all start off by facing a wall whilst standing upright. Your right foot should be close to the wall and your right knee bent. Now place your hands flat against the wall and at a height that is level with your shoulders. Stretch your left leg far out behind you, without lifting your toes and heel off the floor, and lean towards the wall.

Once you have performed this stretch for 25 seconds, switch legs and carry out the same procedure for the right leg. As with all exercises contained within this guide, stop if you feel any pain or discomfort.

Stretching the shoulder muscles
To begin with, stand with your feet slightly apart and with your knees only slightly bent. Now hold your arms right out in front of you, with your palms facing away from you and with your fingers pointing skywards. Now place your right palm on the back of your left hand and use it to push the left hand further away from you. If you are performing this exercise correctly then you will feel the muscles in your shoulder stretching. Hold for 10 seconds before switching sides.

Stretching the quad muscles (front of the thigh)
Before you carry out any form of brisk walking or running, it is imperative that you stretch your leg muscles. During the fitness tests, and especially prior to the multi-stage fitness test, the instructors should take you through a series of warm-up exercises, which will include stretching the quad

muscles. To begin with, stand with your right hand pressed against the back of a wall or firm surface. Bend your left knee and bring your left heel up to your bottom whilst grasping your foot with your left hand. Your back should be straight and your shoulders, hips and knees should all be in line at all times during the exercise. Hold for 25 seconds before switching legs.

Stretching the hamstring muscles (back of the thigh)

To perform this exercise correctly, stand up straight and place your right foot onto a table or other firm surface so that your leg is almost parallel to the floor. Keep your left leg straight and your foot at a right angle to your leg. Start to slowly move your hands down your right leg towards your ankle until you feel tension on the underside of your thigh. When you feel this tension you know that you are starting to stretch the hamstring muscles. Hold for 25 seconds before switching legs.

We have only covered a small number of stretching exercises within this section; however, it is crucial that you stretch out fully in all areas before carrying out any of the following exercises. Remember to obtain professional advice before carrying out any type of exercise.

RUNNING

As I have already mentioned, one of the best ways to prepare for the fitness tests is to embark on a structured running programme. You do not need to run at a fast pace or even run for long distances, in order to gain massively from this type of exercise.

Before I joined the Fire Service I spent a few years in the Royal Navy. I applied to join the Navy when I was 16 and

I made it through the selection process with ease until I reached the medical. During the medical the doctor told me that I was overweight and that I had to lose a stone before they would accept me. To be honest, I was heartbroken. I couldn't believe it; especially after all the hard work I had put in preparing for the tests and the interview! Anyway, as soon as I arrived back home from the medical I started out on a structured running programme that would see me lose the stone in weight within only 4 weeks! The following running programme is very similar to the one I used all those years ago and it will serve you well when preparing for the fitness tests.

Before I provide you with the running programme, however, take a read of the following important running tips.

Tips for running

- As with any exercise, you should consult a doctor before taking part to make sure that you are medically fit.

- It is certainly worth investing in a pair of comfortable running shoes that serve the purpose for your intended training programme. Your local sports shop will be able to advise you on the types that are best for you. You don't have to spend a fortune to buy a good pair of running shoes.

- It is a good idea to invest in a 'high visibility' jacket or coat so that you can be seen by fast moving traffic if you intend to run on or near the road.

- Make sure you carry out at least 5 whole minutes of stretching exercises not only before but also after your running programme. This can help to prevent injury.

- Whilst you shouldn't run on a full stomach, it is also not good to run on an empty one either. A great food to eat

approximately 30 minutes before a run is a banana. This is great for giving you energy.

- Drink plenty of water throughout the day. Try to drink at least 1.5 litres each day in total. This will keep you hydrated and help to prevent muscle cramp.

- Don't overdo it. If you feel any pain or discomfort then stop and seek medical advice.

RUNNING PROGRAMME WEEK 1

Day 1
- Run a total of 3 miles only at a steady pace.

If you cannot manage 3 miles then try the following:
- Walk at a brisk pace for half a mile or approximately 10 minutes.

Then
- Run for 1 mile or 8 minutes.

Then
- Walk for another half a mile or approximately 10 minutes.

Then
- Run for 1.5 miles or 12 minutes.

Walking at a brisk pace is probably the most effective way to lose weight if you need to. It is possible to burn the same amount of calories if you walk the same distance as if you were running.

When walking at a 'brisk' pace it is recommended that you walk as fast as is comfortably possible without breaking into a run or slow jog.

Day 2
- Walk for 2 miles or approximately 20 minutes at a brisk pace.

Then
- Run for 2 miles or 14 minutes.

Day 3
- Repeat DAY ONE.

Day 4

- Walk at a brisk pace for 0.5 miles or approximately 7 minutes.

Then
- Run for 3 miles or 20 minutes.

DAY 5

- Repeat day one.

DAY 6 AND DAY 7

- Rest days. No exercise.

RUNNING PROGRAMME WEEK 2

Day 1
- Run for 4 miles or 25 minutes.

Day2
- Run a total of 3 miles at a steady pace.

If you cannot manage 3 miles then try the following:

- Walk at a brisk pace for half a mile or approximately 10 minutes.

Then
- Run for 1 mile or 8 minutes.

Then
- Walk for another half a mile or approximately 10 minutes.

Then
- Run for 1.5 miles or 12 minutes.

Day 3
- Rest day. No exercise.

Day 4
- Run for 5 miles or 35 - 40 minutes.

Day 5
- Run for 3 miles or 20 minutes.

Then
- Walk at a brisk pace for 2 miles or approximately 20 minutes.

Day 6
- Run for 5 miles or 35 to 45 minutes.

Day 7
- Rest day. No exercise.

Once you have completed the second week running programme, use the third week to perform different types of exercises, such as cycling and swimming. During week 4 you can then commence the 2-week running programme again. You'll be amazed at how much easier it is the second time around!

When preparing for the Prison Officer selection process, use your exercise time as a break from your studies. For example, if you have been working on the application form for a couple of hours, why not take a break and go running? When you return from your run you can then concentrate on your studies feeling refreshed.

Now that I've provided you with a structured running programme to follow, there really are no excuses. So, get out

there and start running! I'll now provide you with a number of key targeted exercises that will allow you to prepare effectively for the fitness tests.

EXERCISES THAT WILL IMPROVE YOUR ABILITY TO PASS THE PRISON OFFICER FITNESS TESTS

Press-ups

Whilst running is a great way to improve your overall fitness, you will also need to carry out exercises that improve your upper body strength. These exercises will help you to pass the strength tests, which form part of the assessment. The great thing about press-ups is that you don't have to attend a gym to perform them. However, you must ensure that you can do them correctly as injury can occur. You only need to spend just 5 minutes every day on press-ups, possibly after you go running or even before if you prefer. If you are not used to doing press-ups then start slowly and aim to carry out at least 10.

Even if you struggle to do just 10, you will soon find that after a few days' practice at these you will be up to 20+.

Step 1 - To begin with, lie on a mat or even surface. Your hands should be shoulder width apart and fully extend the arms.

Step 2 - Gradually lower your body until the elbows reach 90°. Do not rush the movement as you may cause injury.

Step 3 - Once your elbows reach 90° slowly return to the starting position with your arms fully extended.

The press-up action should be a continuous movement with no rest. However, it is important that the exercise is as smooth as possible and there should be no jolting or sudden movements. Try to complete as many press-ups as possible

and always keep a record of how many you do. This will keep you focused and also maintain your motivation levels.

Did you know that the world record for non-stop press-ups is currently 10,507 set in 1980!

WARNING – Ensure you take advice from a competent fitness trainer in relation to the correct execution of press-up exercises and other exercises contained within this guide.

Sit-ups

Sit-ups are great for building the core stomach muscles. At the commencement of the exercise lie flat on your back with your knees bent at a 45° angle and with your feet together. Your hands can either be crossed on your chest, by your sides, or cupped behind your ears.

Without moving your lower body, curl your upper torso upwards and in towards your knees, until your shoulder blades are as high off the ground as possible. As you reach the highest point, tighten your abdominal muscles for a brief second. This will allow you to get the most out of the exercise. Now slowly start to lower yourself back to the starting position. You should be aiming to work up to at least 50 effective sit-ups every day. You will be amazed at how quickly this can be achieved and you will begin to notice your stomach muscles developing.

Whilst sit-ups do not form part of fitness tests, they are still a great way of improving your all-round fitness and therefore should not be neglected.

Pull-ups

Pull-ups are another great way for building the core upper body muscle groups. The unfortunate thing about this type of exercise is you will probably need to attend a gym in order to carry them out. Having said that, there are a number

of different types of 'pull-up bars' available to buy on the market that can easily and safely be fitted to a doorway at home. If you choose to purchase one of these items make sure that it conforms to the relevant safety standards first.

Lateral pull-ups are very effective at increasing upper body strength. If you have access to a gymnasium then these can be practised on a 'lateral pull-up' machine. It is advised that you consult a member of staff at your gym to ask about these exercises.

Pull-ups should be performed by firmly grasping a sturdy and solid bar. Before you grasp the bar make sure it is safe. Your hands should be roughly shoulder width apart. Straighten your arms so that your body hangs loose. You will feel your lateral muscles and biceps stretching as you hang in the air. This is the starting position for the lateral pull-up exercise.

Next, pull yourself upwards to the point where your chest is almost touching the bar and your chin is actually over the bar. Whilst pulling upwards, focus on keeping your body straight without any arching or swinging as this can result in injury. Once your chin is over the bar, you can lower yourself back down to the initial starting position. Repeat the exercise 10 times.

Squats (these work the legs and bottom)

Squats are a great exercise for working the leg muscles. They are the perfect exercise in your preparation for the fitness tests.

At the commencement of the exercise, stand up straight with your arms at your sides. Concentrate on keeping your feet shoulder-width apart and your head up. Do not look downwards at any point during the exercise.

Now start to very slowly bend your knees while pushing

your rear out as though you are about to sit down on a chair. Keep lowering yourself down until your thighs reach past the 90° point. Make sure your weight is on your heels so that your knees do not extend over your toes. At this point you may wish to tighten your thighs and buttocks to intensify the exercise.

As you come back up to a standing position, push down through your heels, which will allow you to maintain your balance. Repeat the exercise 15 to 20 times.

Lunges (these work the thighs and bottom)

You will have noticed throughout this section of the guide that I have been providing you with simple, yet highly effective exercises that can be carried out at home. The lunge exercise is another great addition to the range of exercises that require no attendance at the gym.

To begin with, stand with your back straight and your feet together (you may hold light hand weights if you wish to add some intensity to the exercise).

Next, take a big step forward as illustrated in the above diagram, making sure you inhale as go and landing with the heel first. Bend the front knee no more than 90 degrees so as to avoid injury. Keep your back straight and lower the back knee as close to the floor as possible. Your front knee should be lined up over your ankle and your back thigh should be in line with your back.

To complete the exercise, exhale and push down against your front heel, squeezing your buttocks tight as you rise back to the starting position.

Try to repeat the exercise 15 to 20 times before switching sides.

Lateral raises (these work the shoulder muscles)

Whilst Prison Officers are not usually required to lift heavy items of equipment during their day-to-day work, they still need to have a good level of upper body strength in order to carry out Control and Restraint (C & R) procedures. Lateral raises will allow you improve your upper body strength in a safe and effective manner.

Take a dumbbell in each hand and hold them by the sides of your body with your palms facing inward.

Stand or sit with your feet shoulder-width apart, knees slightly bent. Do not lean backwards as you could cause injury to your back. Raise your arms up and out to the sides until they are parallel to the ground, then lower them back down carefully. Repeat the exercise 15 to 20 times.

ALTERNATIVE EXERCISES

Swimming

Apart from press-ups, lateral raises and the other exercises I have provided you with, another fantastic way to improve your upper body and overall fitness is to go swimming. If you have access to a swimming pool, and you can swim, then this is a brilliant way to improve your fitness.

If you are not a great swimmer you can start off with short distances and gradually build up your swimming strength and stamina. Breaststroke is sufficient for building good upper body strength providing you put the effort into swimming an effective number of lengths. You may wish to alternate your running programme with the odd day of swimming. If you can swim 10 lengths of a 25-metre pool initially then this is a good base to start from. You will soon find that you can increase this number easily providing that you carry on swimming every week. Try running to your local

swimming pool, if it is not too far away, swimming 20 lengths of breaststroke, and then running back home.

This is a great way to combine your fitness activity and prevent yourself from becoming bored of your training programme.

Rowing

If there is one exercise that will allow you to work every single muscle group in the body then it is rowing. This is the perfect exercise for preparing to pass the fitness tests. It will increase your aerobic fitness and it will also improve your lower and upper body strength.

As with any exercise of this nature there is a risk of injury. It is crucial that you use the correct technique when rowing on a purpose built machine. By applying the correct technique you will be far more efficient and you will also see faster results.

Whilst exercising on the rowing machine, make sure you keep your back straight and concentrate on using your legs and buttocks. Never extend so far that you lock out your knees. Try to be smooth throughout the entire exercise. To obtain a suitable indoor rowing training programme that is relevant to your current fitness levels please visit www.concept2.co.uk.

The Multi-Stage Fitness Test or Bleep Test

This part of the Prison Officer selection process requires you to demonstrate a specific level of fitness.

In simple terms the bleep test requires you to run backwards and forwards (shuttles) between 2 fixed points a set distance apart. The test is progressive in that as the levels increase so does the difficulty. A tape will be played that contains a series of 'bleeps' set out at different intervals.

The distance between the 'bleeps' at level 1 will be far greater than the 'bleeps' at level 10. Each time the 'bleeps' increase, the tape will let you know that you are progressing to the next level. During the test you will be required to keep up with 'bleeps' and not fall behind them or run ahead of them. Level 1 starts off at around walking pace and gradually increases as each stage progresses.

The best way to practise for this stage of the test is to practise the actual test itself. However, the next best alternative is to go running for at least 3 miles, at least 3 times a week. Each time you go out running you should try to push yourself a little bit harder and further.

By running 3 times a week you will give your body the rest it needs in between each run so it is probably best to run on alternate days.

TIPS FOR STAYING WITH YOUR WORKOUT

The hardest part of your training programme will be sticking with it. In this final section of your fitness guide I will provide some useful golden rules that will enable you to maintain your motivational levels in the build up to the Prison Officer tests. In order to stay with your workout for longer, try following these simple rules:

Golden rule number one - Work out often
Aim to train three to five times each and every week.

Each training session should last between 20 minutes to a maximum of an hour. The quality of training is important so don't go for heavy weights but instead go for a lighter weight with a better technique. On days when you are feeling energetic, take advantage of this opportunity and do more!

Within this guide I have deliberately provided you with a number of 'simple-to-perform' exercises that are targeted at the core muscle groups required to perform the role of a Prison Officer. In between your study sessions try carrying out these exercises at home or get yourself out on the road running or cycling. Use your study 'down-time' effectively and wisely.

Golden rule number two - Mix up your exercises

Your exercise programme should include some elements of cardiovascular (aerobics, running, brisk walking and cycling), resistance training (weights or own body exercises such as press-ups and sit-ups) and, finally, flexibility (stretching). Make sure that you always warm-up and warm-down.

If you are a member of a gym then consider taking up a class such as Pilates. This form of exercise class will teach you how to build core training into your exercise principles, and show you how to hit your abdominals in ways that are not possible with conventional sit-ups. If you are a member of a gym then a fantastic 'all-round' exercise that I strongly recommend is rowing. Rowing will hit every major muscle group in your body and it is also perfect for improving your stamina levels and cardiovascular fitness.

Golden rule number three - Eat a healthy and balanced diet

It is vitally important that you eat the right fuel to give you the energy to train to your full potential. Don't fill your body with rubbish and then expect to train well. Think about what you are eating and drinking, including the quantities, and keep a record of what you are digesting. You will become stronger and fitter more quickly if you eat little amounts of nutritious foods at short intervals.

Golden rule number four - Get help

Try working with a personal trainer. They will ensure that you work hard and will help you to achieve your goals. If you cannot afford a personal trainer then try training with someone else. The mere fact that they are there at your side will add an element of competition to your training sessions!

A consultation with a professional nutritionist will also help you improve your eating habits and establish your individual food needs.

Golden rule number five - Fitness is for life

One of my old managers in the Fire Service had a saying – "Fitness Wins!" Two simple words that meant an awful lot. Improving your fitness and eating healthily are not short-term projects. They are things that should come naturally to you.

Make fitness a permanent part of your life by following these tips, and you'll lead a better and more fulfilling life!

Good luck and work hard to improve your weak areas.

A FEW FINAL WORDS

You have now reached the end of the guide and no doubt you will be ready to start preparing for the selection process. Just before you go off and start on your preparation, consider the following.

The majority of candidates who pass the selection process have a number of common attributes. These are as follows:

1. They believe in themselves.
The first factor is self-belief. Regardless of what anyone tells you, you can become a Prison Officer. Just like any job of this nature, you have to be prepared to work hard in order to be successful. Make sure you have the self-belief to pass the selection process and fill your mind with positive thoughts.

2. They prepare fully.
The second factor is preparation. Those people who achieve in life prepare fully for every eventuality and that is what you must do when you apply to become a Prison Officer. Work very hard and especially concentrate on your weak areas.

3. They persevere.
Perseverance is a fantastic word. Everybody comes across obstacles or setbacks in their life, but it is what you do about those setbacks that is important. If you fail at something, then ask yourself 'why' you have failed. This will allow you to improve for next time and if you keep improving and trying, success will eventually follow. Apply this same method of thinking when you apply to become a Prison Officer.

4. They are self-motivated.
How much do you want this job? Do you want it, or do you really want it?

When you apply to join the Prison Service you should want it more than anything in the world. Your levels of self-motivation will shine through during the assessments. For the weeks and months leading up to the selection process, be motivated as best you can and always keep your fitness levels up as this will serve to increase your levels of motivation.

Work hard, stay focused and be what you want…

Richard McMunn

Visit www.how2become.co.uk to find more titles and courses that will help you to pass the Prison Officer selection process, including:

- How to pass the Prison Officer Role-Play DVD.

- 1-Day Prison Officer training course.

- Online Prison Officer Selection Test.

- Psychometric testing books and CDs.

www.how2become.co.uk